P9-AFF-091

All I Need to Know in Life I Learned From Romance Novels

Publisher: W. Quay Hays
Editor: Dana Stibor
Designer: Dana Granoski
Jacket design: Chitra Sekhar

Copyright © 1998 by Victoria M. Johnson

All rights reserved under International and Pan-American Copyright
Conventions. This book, or any parts thereof, may not be reproduced in any
fashion whatsoever without the prior written permission of the Publisher.

For information:
General Publishing Group, Inc.
2701 Ocean Park Boulevard, Suite 140
Santa Monica, CA 90405

Library of Congress Cataloging-in-Publication Data

Johnson, Victoria M.
    All I need to know in life I learned from romance novels / by
Victoria M. Johnson : introduction by Phyllis Taylor Pianka.
        p.   cm.
    ISBN 1-57544-101-2
    1. Love stories, American--History and criticism.   2. Love
stories, American--Bibliography.   3. Love stories--Appreciation.
4. Women--Books and reading.   I. Title.
PS374.L6J64   1998
813'.08509--dc21   98-34394
                                                                    CIP

Printed in the USA by RR Donnelley & Sons Company
10 9 8 7 6 5 4 3 2 1

General Publishing Group
Los Angeles

Dedication

To my dashing husband, Michael, whose love, encouragement, toughness, and sense of humor helped me become a writer. To my marvelous children, Michelle, Justin, and Sabrina, who inspired me to follow my dreams.

To my mother, Frances, whose inner strength and big heart showed me what real heroines are made of.

For Melissa McClone and Linda Hill, special friends and romance writers extraordinaire. For my writing friends, Phyllis, Elaine, Pam, Kristen, Mary Ann, Kathy, Kay, and Dina...thanks for your high standards and enthusiasm.

To romance writers everywhere for their devotion to bringing the world stories of hope, love, courage, and romance. The world would be a dreary place without romance.

Acknowledgments

Special thanks, from the bottom of my heart, to all the gracious and talented writers who contributed their words of wisdom by way of original quotes included in this book:

Joyce Adams

Rosalyn Alsobrook

Jo Beverley

Dixie Browning

Stella Cameron

Casey Claybourne

Jennifer Crusie

Daphne Clair de Jong

Jude Deveraux

Anne Marie Duquette

Kathleen Eagle

JoAnn Ferguson

Vanessa Grant

Jennifer Greene

Shirley Hailstock

Linda Hill

Karen Leabo

Kat Martin

Melissa Martinez McClone

Teresa Medeiros

Leigh Michaels

Susan Plunkett

Francis Ray

Renee Roszel

Amanda Scott

Barbara Dawson Smith

Cheryl St. John

Janelle Taylor

Elizabeth Thornton

Kathleen E. Woodiwiss

Also to Phyllis Taylor Pianka for contributing the Introduction.

Permissions

A very appreciative thank you to the following authors and publishers for granting permission to reprint excerpts from the following novels:

Avon Books

Daniels' Gift by Barbara Freethy. Copyright © 1996 by Barbara Freethy. Used with permission of Avon Books.

Almost A Lady by Sonya Birmingham. Copyright © 1993 by Sonya Birmingham. Used with permission of Avon Books.

Ballantine Books

Tigress by Jennifer Blake. Copyright ©1996 by Patricia Maxwell. Used with permission of Fawcett Gold Medal–Ballantine Books.

Bantam Doubleday Dell

Keeper of the Dream by Penelope Williamson. Published by Dell. Copyright © 1992 by Penelope Williamson.

Night of the Panther by Suzanne Forster. Bantam Loveswept # 581, published by Bantam. Copyright © 1992 by Suzanne Forster.

Outlander by Diana Gabaldon. Published by Delacorte. Copyright © 1991 by Diana Gabaldon.

The Perfect Mistress by Betina Krahn. Published by Bantam. Copyright © 1995 by Betina Krahn.

Prince of Wolves by Susan Krinard. Published by Bantam. Copyright © 1994 by Susan Krinard.

Dorchester Publishing Co., Inc.

Apollo's Fault by Miriam Raftery. Published by Dorchester Publishing Co., Inc. Copyright © 1996 by Miriam Raftery. Used with permission.

Midnight Rose by Robin Lee Hatcher. Published by Dorchester Publishing Co., Inc. Copyright © 1992 by Robin Lee Hatcher. Used with permission.

Penguin Putnam Inc.

A Touch Of Lace by Margaret Brownley. Copyright © 1996 by Margaret Brownley. Used by perission of Dutton, a division of Penguin Putnam Inc.

The Heir by Catherine Coulter. Copyright © 1980, 1996 by Catherine Coulter. Used by permission of Dutton Signet, a division of Penguin Putnam Inc.

Mad, Bad & Dangerous to Know by Mary Jo Putney. Copyright © 1993 by Mary Jo Putney. Used by permission of Dutton Signet, a division of Penguin Putnam Inc.

Harlequin Enterprises

Hunk Of The Month, Temptation #683, by JoAnn Ross. Used with permission. Copyright © 1998 by JoAnn Ross.

The Wedding Night, Temptation #365, by Jayne Ann Krentz. Used with permission. Copyright © 1991 by Jayne Ann Krentz.

The Mighty Quinn, Temptation #397, by Candace Schuler. Used with permission. Copyright © 1992 by Candace Schuler.

Yesterday's Secrets, Superromance #567, by Tara Taylor Quinn. Used with permission. Copyright © 1993 by Tara Lee Reames.

A River To Cross, Special Edition #910, by Laurie Paige. Used with permission. Copyright © 1994 by Olivia M. Hall.

On Middle Ground, Special Edition #772, by Sierra Rydell. Used with permission. Copyright © 1992 by Ramona Rolle-Berg.

Three Brides, No Groom, Silhouette, by Debbie Macomber. Used with permission. Copyright © 1997 by Debbie Macomber.

Home Is Where The Heart Is, Romance #882, by Carol Grace. Used with permission. Copyright © 1992 by Carol Culver.

Mail-Order Male, Romance #955, by Carol Grace. Used with permission. Copyright © 1993 by Carol Culver.

The Man Behind The Magic, Romance #950, by Kristina Logan. Used with permission. Copyright © 1993 by Barbara Beharry Freathy.

Wife For a Night, Desire #1118, by Carol Grace. Used with permission. Copyright © 1998 by Carol Culver.

Switched At The Altar, Desire #1133, by Metsy Hingle. Used with permission. Copyright © 1998 by Metsy Hingle.

A Man For Amanda, Silhouette Desire #649, Copyright © 1991 by Nora Roberts. All rights reserved. Reproduction with permission of the publisher Harlequin Books S.A.

Harlequin Books: Mills & Boon

Permission to reprint extracts from the following works granted by Harlequin Books S.A.:

One Love Forever, Harlequin Romance #131, by Barbara McMahon. Copyright © 1992 by Barbara McMahon.

Thunder Over Eden, Harlequin Romance #83, by Emma Goldrick. Copyright © 1985 by Emma Goldrick.

Return To Sender, Harlequin Romance #3390, by Rebecca Winters. Copyright © 1995 by Rebecca Winters.

Second-Best Wife, Harlequin Romance #3460, by Rebecca Winters. Copyright © 1996 by Rebecca Winters.

His Cinderella Bride, Harlequin Romance #3466, by Heather Allison. Copyright © 1996 by Heather W. MacAllister.

The Glass Madonna by Liza Manning. Published by Mills & Boon, Harlequin Romance #2818. Copyright © 1986 by Liza Manning. Used with permission of Laurence Pollinger Limited and Liza Manning.

HarperCollins Publishers, Inc.

Something's Cooking by Joanne Pence. Copyright © 1993 by Joanne Pence.

Kensington Publishing Corp.

Reprinted by permission from *An Intriguing Affair*. Copyright © 1993 by Mary Kingsley. Published by Zebra Books, an imprint of Kensington Publishing Corp.

Reprinted by permission from *A Man In Uniform*, Precious Gem #77. Copyright © 1997 by Cynthia Van Rooy. Published by Zebra Books, an imprint of Kensington Publishing Corp.

Reprinted by permission from *Reunited*, Precious Gem #137. Copyright © 1998 by Jan Scarbrough. Published by Zebra Books, an imprint of Kensington Publishing Corp.

Simon & Schuster

Reprinted with permission of Pocket Books, a division of Simon & Schuster, from *Wildest Hearts*. Copyright © 1993 by Jayne Ann Krentz.

Reprinted with permission of Pocket Books, a division of Simon & Schuster, from *Carried Away* by Jill Barnett. Copyright © 1996 by Jill Barnett Stadler.

Reprinted with permission of Pocket Books, a division of Simon & Schuster, from *Wild Heart* by Jane Bonander. Copyright © 1995 by Jane Bonander.

Reprinted with the permission of Simon & Schuster from *The Outsider* by Penelope Williamson. Copyright © 1996 by Penelope Williamson.

Other Acknowledgments

The following novels are referred to in this book but permissions were not required.

Reckless Love, by Ann Maxwell, Harlequin

Tomorrow Come Soon, by Jessica Steele, Harlequin #2607

The Mermaid Wife, by Rebecca Winters, Harlequin #3312

Breath Of Scandal, by Sandra Brown, Warner Books

A Knight In Shining Armor, by Jude Deveraux, Pocket Books

A Man To Remember, by Jodi O'Donnell, Silhouette #1021

The Forgotten Husband, by Elizabeth August, Silhouette #1019

Nobody's Baby But Mine, by Susan Elizabeth Phillips, Avon Books

Bewitching, by Jill Barnett, Pocket Books

Walking After Midnight, by Karen Robards, Delacorte Press

Say You Love Me, by Johanna Lindsey, Avon Books

Contents

Foreword

With words alone, romance writers grab us and pull us along on the all-absorbing experience of falling in love. Romance novels show people at their best and their worst, at their strongest and their most vulnerable.

But what makes millions of readers worldwide turn to romance novels? Is there something about them that rings true for real life? You bet there is! This book compiles the good sense I've learned from reading thousands of these cleverly written books. There is a multitude of wisdom within the pages of romance novels—subtle lessons that apply to life and that motivate readers to strive to be their best in their own lives.

This book applauds the significant, optimistic veracity of romance novels. Enjoy!

Introduction

By Phyllis Taylor Pianka

I first began reading romance novels as a young girl. Grace Livingston Hill's books, based on Christian living, sweet heroines, and gentle yet strong heroes, were popular then and I read every book I could find.

There was no doubt in my mind that these heroes and heroines were idealized characters. What woman would fall in love with a man simply because he left a white rose on her chair in the choir loft? What sensible woman would fall in love with a man the first time she saw him?

Yet from the moment I met my future husband, I knew that he was the man for me. I was right.

During the ensuing years, romance novels have evolved along with the changing role of women in society. In the '70s, romance novel heroines were young and virginal nurses, teachers, or secretaries, destined to give up their pursuits to become homemakers. Heroes were father figures, they were macho, handsome, and, above all, rich.

As the demand for romance novels increased, writers began to realize that women wanted more realistic stories. Stories about struggles and hardships, stories about babies, and about strong women and heroes to die for. At the same time they wanted stories that retained an element of fantasy. Women had found their roots; now they wanted wings.

Like today's women, heroines in romance novels were offered choices; a banquet of opportunities, along with the necessary courage to step up to the table and ask for what they wanted.

Perhaps the most valuable lesson that women have learned from romance novels is that we can do anything, be anything, if we have a need and the desire to accept the challenge.

But it is not women alone who have learned life's lessons from romance novels. Men, too, have become romance readers as well as romance writers. One man once said to me that he never realized what women really wanted from a man until he read his wife's romance novel on the train to the city. "It was wrapped in brown paper," he admitted with a grin. Nowadays it's not so uncommon to see a man reading romances.

And why should it be? Love and commitment are basic human needs. Romance novels are a celebration of love. And love, along with commitment, symbolizes all that is good in this world.

Romance novels give us hope: hope for the future, hope for the present. For a few moments we can escape our mundane lives and read of someone else whose problems will be solved and the ending will be happy. If we're lucky, the story will be remembered with a smile.

—**Jude Deveraux**

I'm not so much a romantic as an idealist, and that's what I like about romance novels. They present the world as it could be—a place where people really communicate and care about each other, a place where in the end everything works out just right. A beautiful world—that I'd really like to live in!

—Leigh Michaels

Never judge a book by its cover

1

"You needn't be afraid to tell me the truth," he coaxed...
"Despite your wanton behavior, I won't send you back."
"Back where?" I asked, startled.
"To the bordello you've run away from."
"Is that what you think?" I said aghast. Okay so I'd
flirted with the guy—that didn't give him the right
to treat me like a prostitute. The nerve.

—**Miriam Raftery, Apollo's Fault**

We've all seen them—those risqué illustrations overflowing with muscles and bosoms, long hair cascading down bare shoulders, a breeze blowing from somewhere offstage, a horse looking out of place. Then, after we read the book, we have no idea where the cover came from—especially the horse.

I used to be fooled by those racy book covers. I'd avoid those books, thinking they definitely would not be my kind of story. Besides, I wasn't brave enough to take a sexy looking novel to the check-out counter, knowing I'd be embarrassed by the condescending glances I might receive. And I was afraid the ridicule would continue once I got the book home. My family had never made fun of my romance novels, but I'd never brought one home with that kind of cover. What would I say to my teenage daughter? She'd roll her eyes no matter what I said. My husband might wonder why I felt I 'needed' such a book. My palms felt damp, my throat thick, just thinking about the imaginary conversations.

Thankfully, the time came when I got over it. An author I admire wrote a book that happened to be graced with a voluptuously brazen cover, horse and all. I trusted that author's gift of story-telling, and not wanting to miss her newest release, I took a chance.

That's when I discovered a hidden truth of romance novels: The cover had nothing to do with the story—it wasn't associated with the premise, theme, or even the characters. The exterior actually concealed the interior. The puzzle became a revelation—the artist didn't read the book! Now, I wonder how many wonderful stories I've missed, and I wonder if the same is true of people. How many people have I avoided thinking they would not fit into my kind of crowd?

So for both romance novels and people, you can't tell what's on the inside by looking at the outside because appearances can be deceiving. In romance novels, the hero and heroine sometimes meet in a situation where one or the other's intentions are misunderstood. Sometimes there's no interaction and assumptions are made on appearances alone. As their stories unfold, they realize they were wrong about the other person.

In Ann Maxwell's book *Reckless Love*, the hero thinks he's protecting a boy in the Wild West, only to find that the heroine has dressed like a boy to survive on the open frontier. In Robin Lee Hatcher's story *Midnight Rose*, the hero learns that the genteel lady he loves is also the masked leader of a pack of *hombres*. In Jessica Steele's *Tomorrow Come Soon*, the hero assumes he is blackmailing a spoiled, jet-setting, wanton woman. Instead, the heroine is a par-tially disabled, kind lady. In Rebecca Winter's *The Mermaid Wife*, the hero is sure the heroine is a genuine mermaid, though the truth is far from his belief.

Heroines have been mistaken for prostitutes, thieves, gold-diggers, and worse; just as heroes have been mistaken for traitors, outlaws, playboys, and the like. Because things often aren't what they seem to be, looking beyond first impressions is vital. Our characters learn the hard way that what you see on the surface isn't important; it's what's on the inside that counts. And with a person, as with a romance novel, what's inside just might bring you excitement, happiness, and warm memories to last a lifetime.

Unlike other forms of fiction, romance novels spotlight a woman who struggles but always wins in the end. I can count on a romance to feature a strong heroine who is capable of being an equal mate to her man. But what I like best is the celebration of love, commitment, and positive values. If everyone would read romances, the world would be a better place!

—**Barbara Dawson Smith**

No one is going to rescue you—you have to rescue yourself

2

> *She managed to reach the trail, drained of*
> *energy and feeling as if she had nothing left.*
> *Somehow she kept going, but it was on nerves*
> *alone. She kept moving, knowing if she stopped,*
> *she would collapse in a heap and never move again.*
>
> **—Suzanne Forster, Night of the Panther**

A common misconception about romance novels goes something like this: A man charges in on a white horse, swoops up the heroine, and rides off into the sunset, thus freeing her from all her problems and rescuing her from a dull, loveless future. This stereotype is delightfully untrue in the modern romance novel.

The modern romance novel heroine never, ever, waits around to be rescued. Whether she's a medieval maiden, an Old West pioneer, a regency lady, or a contemporary woman, she has goals in her life, and a purpose. The novel often begins when something or someone has interfered with the heroine reaching her goal. These stumbling blocks are anything but mundane and have a major impact on her destiny. The heroine now must regroup, make decisions, and set forward on her course once again.

Her goal may be altered as she faces obstacles; she may be side-tracked. Meeting the hero will certainly upset her perfectly laid plans. Like any man, he always has his own goals.

When his goals oppose hers, the conflict builds. They clash, they antagonize each other, their motives are challenged. We know neither one of them will come out of this encounter unchanged.

But the heroine remains true to her purpose. It defines who she is inside, what she's all about in her heart. It's the driving force that propels her to get up every morning and pushes her to take action, to do something.

Despite what life throws at the heroine, she always pulls through. She hangs on just a little bit longer, tries just one more time, and vows to give it all she's got. She's not waiting for a man, but for her circumstances to improve, for her luck to change, for her efforts to succeed, or to die before giving up.

See for yourself with Jennifer Blake's *Tigress*, where the heroine must rely on herself for survival. "It was up to her. There was no one else. Her best chance might come from being a woman. Holliwell considered her weak and defenseless, so he was supremely confident of his control of the situation. That meant the element of surprise would be on her side."

The hero comes to know the heroine's nature through the course of the relationship, even an uncertain relationship. He sees her fighting spirit, her intelligence, her inner beauty.

Because the hero learns what is important to the heroine and sees her fighting for it, he learns what makes her tick. How else can the hero fall completely in love with her? He gets to know the real woman. Even if they started out the story as rivals or enemies, they can end up being soul mates.

In life, how many women find a soul mate by being a doormat or a pushover? Only women true to themselves find their true soul mates. Women who are busy living their lives or striving toward their purpose are more likely to find what (and whom) they want than women who expect others to be their road to success. Sometimes the heroine's goal is to ensure the betterment or safety of others. That's when they unexpectedly find love, while rescuing themselves or someone else.

Don't wait to be rescued. The man who rides up on his white horse may not be the one destined for you. Go out and make your own destiny. You may win even more than you imagined.

There are wonderful books in every writing field, but one of the reasons I was drawn to writing romance was because of the unique personal relationship between the writer and reader. I always feel like I'm writing to a sister...someone who's struggling with all the different women's roles today, as I am...someone who believes in commitment and healthy relationships and families, as I do. We share secrets and fears. We share problems. We also share beliefs about what really matters in life. And yes, we do this through the medium of a love story—but we also reach out a helping hand to each other through our stories.

—Jennifer Greene

Marriage is still a wonderful institution

3

> *Now, he believed that Diego was the one man who*
> *could make his sister happy, the one man strong*
> *enough for his strong-willed sister. He hoped*
> *he was right. "Amigo, if you want a meek wife*
> *who will blindly obey and look to you to do her*
> *thinking for her, don't marry Leona, I beg you.*
> *You'll only make her unhappy, and she'll make*
> *you miserable."*
>
> **—Robin Lee Hatcher, Midnight Rose**

Marriage has received bad publicity over the years. For some, marriages come and go with the fads of clothing—they change spouses faster than hem lengths change styles. These couples give marriage a bad name.

But there are millions more who give marriage a good name. These couples hang on in tough times and savor the happy times. They support one another through the storms. They give their spouses strength. The world is a scary place and having a partner to share worries with is a blessing. Marriage brings us a sense of security; we are not alone. The world can also be an exciting place, and having someone to share discoveries with is precious.

But marriages do more than that. Marriages are the foundation of families, and families are the foundation of society. What would society be without the family structure? We'd have no one taking responsibility for raising our young; not just feeding and clothing them—an institution can do that—but also teaching them to understand right from wrong, to think independently, to be creative, to chase dreams. Who would give them encouragement or affection? How would they learn values, family traditions, and that making mistakes is a part of life?

Families are as varied as the stars in the sky. The result is a mixture of opinions, colors, flavors, adventures, and clothing accessories. Individual family guidelines are enforced; love and values are taught. But as a larger unit, a community, the values tend to be the same, resulting in a cohesive environment where basic rules of society are followed. So families give communities security and stability.

The family unit also gives motivation for the parents to succeed. They want to give their children things: a warm house, food on the table, a higher education, electronic games and CDs. Most of us would rather not work! We'd love to lie on the beach sipping margaritas, but having a family to support makes us behave responsibly.

Children give us hope for the future. We have something to look forward to: our child's first steps, followed by kindergarten, high school graduation, college, a career, marriage, and hopefully grandchildren. The cycle continues. While they are growing up, our children do little things that make us smile, make us proud, make us understand the meaning of life. In the process, they learn to have their own hopes and responsibilities.

Since many romance novels end in marriage, is it any wonder they give readers hope for the future? Hope that society, berserk as it may seem at times, will survive. Because families are the single most important unit in the world, and always will be. A marriage joins people together, and marriages and families hold a civilization together. By choosing to marry, we affirm our faith not only in love and romance, but in society.

There is no power on earth like romantic love. It can move mountains; it can exalt us, humble us, transform us. Romances are heroic myths written by women for women. These are stories of female empowerment. In romances, the female protagonist _is_ the hero. What woman can resist that combination?

P.S. I haven't read a thriller or a murder-mystery that couldn't be improved by adding a romance.

—**Elizabeth Thornton**

The secret to hot sex is trust

4

> She looked at him with so much love, he felt
> as if he were floating on a cloud. "It's all
> right, Gunnar. You can unbuckle the sheath,"
> she whispered. He recognized the gesture for
> what it was: an act of faith and trust on her
> part. Gunnar had once envied her uncle because
> of her belief in him. Now, he felt humbled by
> the look of trust in her eyes. Never did he think it
> possible to love anyone as much as he loved her at
> that moment.
>
> **—Margaret Brownley, Touch of Lace**

Passionate lovemaking is more emotional than physical. It's the emotional bond, the total trust in each other that allows a person to expose his or her soul. By the time some people figure this out, they're too old to do anything about it. Yet it's so obvious. A trusting relationship leads to more freely giving of yourself.

Have you ever read about mediocre sex in a romance novel? Not likely. Sexy romance novels showcase glorious, earthshaking, mind-boggling, life-changing sex. However, the sex doesn't usually occur until the heroine is ready. Stories where the hero has been through torment and many cold showers before enjoying himself are particularly fun. Not that the heroine is a tease or strings him along, but she doesn't give him what he wants right away. That's how the dance has been played for centuries—excluding the time of cavemen, of course.

Nor are there many romance novels with gratuitous sex. By the time the characters have intercourse, they are emotionally involved. They may not have admitted their love or verbally committed to one another but, innately, there's a sense of trust. The sex is great. It bonds them closer and is their way of showing each other how much they care. The heroine, who's afraid to speak the words, thinks that the hero knows how much she loves him. But he just thinks she's great in bed, afraid to hope that maybe she does love him. The words go unspoken a little longer, while pent-up feelings explode in bed.

The truly fantastic sex comes after they've crossed the line, when there is trust in the person *and* in the permanence of the relationship. Once our heroine knows this man loves her and wouldn't hurt her, she gives herself entirely to him—mind, body, heart, and soul. The hero's perception of the heroine transforms from carnal desire to indelible need to burning love. These absorbing scenes in the book aren't about body parts reacting automatically, they're about the feelings involved for both parties. The love scenes focus on the depth of consuming emotions that sweep the hero and heroine into total ecstasy and the discovery of each other's core.

Naturally, there's a change in the relationship. Any wrongdoing by a character after their sexual encounter is heightened to a level of betrayal. How could he do that after what we shared? Maybe it didn't mean as much to him as it did to me. Doubts rise. It's now or never for our characters. They must verbalize their feelings for each other and for their relationship. To our relief, they do.

Like in romance novels, the secret to fabulous sex is love that evolves into trust. Or is it trust that evolves into love? It's both. So remember, trust is the best aphrodisiac.

Romance is all around us. All we have to do is look for it. Romance novels are keys to the heart, helping us find ways to unlock the romantic nature that lies within each one of us.

—**Kat Martin**

5
Opposites attract

*She liked mannered, genteel men who were worldly
and polished—men who could toss out a bon mot or
devastating put-down in the cleverest of ways, men
who lived in a world of elegance and took it as
their due. A number of doctors, CEOs, and even a
judge were among her coterie of suitors, and she
thought them all just fine. Inspector Paavo Smith
was completely different... They had nothing in
common, nothing to talk about.*

—Joanne Pence, Something's Cooking

There seems to be an unspoken consensus that opposites attract. Some romance novelists market their books this way. The cover blurb states that she craves a hot-blooded man to melt her cold heart. We've read stories where the sparks fly and fireworks ignite when opposites get together. Royalty and commoner, right-brained and left-brained, reckless and cautious, arrogant and humble. This thinking reinforces the idea that opposites attract. It may be true, but as the novel progresses we find that two people who seemed like night and day actually have much in common.

How does a city slicker attract a country farmer? Why does a ruthless Wall Street investor marry a kindergarten teacher? How does a professional nurse end up with a motorcycle mechanic? What would a heroine with an attaché case and chic suits see in a jeans-clad carpenter? They appear to have nothing in common.

When we read about a hero and heroine from opposite sides of the spectrum, often these differences are in appearance, background, financial status, family, education, or profession. Yet these are not the important things upon which long-term relationships depend. They see beyond the obvious in each other. Instinctively, they know a kindred spirit. Let's examine these characters' characters.

Their true differences end up being in superficial areas of life. Whether one wants to watch wrestling and the other a comedy series, or one wants to go shopping and the other wants to read the paper at home, these are petty contrasts—contradictory ideas about clothing, job choices, or leisure activities don't make a difference. Even social standing and life experiences may not be fundamental concerns in matters of the heart.

As long as values and principles are the same, people can have a match made in heaven. If two people who unite seem the antithesis of each other, look closer. You'll see they have the same deep-rooted beliefs and philosophy of life. They are two people who wouldn't dream of cheating on a spouse, taxes, or their dog. They wouldn't burn the American flag any more than their own house. They believe in personal responsibility and things like loyalty, sharing, and integrity. Maybe they believe in celebrating the Christmas holiday without exchanging gifts. Suddenly the fact that he's a beer-and-pizza guy or that she's a caviar-and-champagne woman becomes less significant.

In Jan Scarbrough's book *Reunited*, the hero and heroine seem to have grown too far apart to ever get back together. Jon says, "...the last time we worked together, you told me where to go." Casey narrowed her eyes, "You can still go there, as far as I'm concerned..." Julia cleared her throat, "Maybe I'd better leave you two alone to settle your differences."

These special couples come to an understanding and learn to compromise in inconsequential areas of life. People who originally seemed like opposites actually make a nice match.

A couple is unmatched when their basic belief systems differ. It's unbelievable if characters are attracted who have opposing views as their core values. That's why the land developer and environmentalist stories don't work. It doesn't matter if they have great sex or other interests in common. If their ideals are contradictory, the relationship will have trouble sooner or later—big trouble, because our values are tested every day.

Sometimes society can take everything away from us, except our principles, and they are all we have to build on. In romance novels, the heroine and hero leave us with the sense that they will stay together regardless of what life throws at them. That's how we know they are perfect allies. They aren't so different after all.

When those little annoyances of your mate have you wondering if you married the right guy, remind yourself of the big things you do have in common. Similarities in values are what make you soul mates: like minds, like hearts.

For me Romance is the mother genre. Romance embraces facets of all other fiction forms and is read by the most adventurous readers there are. We are readers and writers on a quest not only for great stories, but for great stories that help us understand ourselves as deeply sensitive, sensual, and loving creatures.

This is the fiction that finally gave women an opportunity to see themselves through women's eyes (a reflection of their own eyes) rather than exclusively through those of men, or those of women for whom validation rests in competing with men.

Now we begin to see the true wonder of this genre we adore. Not only are women fascinated by its revelations, but men are also becoming intrigued—men who are secure in their masculinity and who seek truly intimate and enduring relationships with women. Through romance in its many forms, men are learning more about how women think, and they are learning that here is a fiction that allows them to fully experience their own sensitivity.

—**Stella Cameron**

Hardworking, successful, charming men are still in demand

6

> *Clark was Nelson Lord's computer wizard. A man so left-brain he walked with a limp. Throughout her college career, Carol had secretly admired his genius... He'd done well for himself. Very well.*
>
> **—Debbie Macomber, Three Brides, No Groom**

With all the male bashing going on in this country, romance novels are one place left in America where a hardworking, successful, rich man is still considered a hero, and romance novels are read by millions of readers each year. That tells me these fine men are still in demand.

Just as the competition is stiff for the hero in a romance novel, the competition is horrendous in life. A wealthy man will always have a string of hopeful ladies admiring and wanting him. What makes him attractive besides the money?

A hero has many desirable attributes. He has a fantastic body and is a phenomenal lover. He may have a prominent name. He shows kindness to others. He is responsible and may have great kids. But these aren't the things that draw women to him, because true heroes aren't made by body type or name, but by character. A man can be kind and responsible but have no personality.

It's a man's zest for life, his drive, his initiative that make him interesting. He has a passion for his profession, he treats women with respect, he's intelligent and has a sense of humor. He's worked for his success. Even if he inherited his money, he works hard to preserve it, grow it, put it to good use. And he doesn't mind when his mate spends his money on herself—isn't that refreshing?

But all the success and money in the world can't buy happiness. Are there other aspects to the man that make him a hero? Absolutely.

Although he's rich, he doesn't look down on people who have less money. He isn't class conscious. His intended companions are, and that's what eliminates them from the running as a suitable wife. They don't get it. But our heroine does. Often she's from a lower economic class herself. Sometimes the hero started in the lower class and worked his way up. He respects where he came from, vowing not to return. If knocked down, he trusts that he can get back up and do it all over again.

Here's how Kristina Logan describes the hero in *The Man Behind The Magic*. "'...Alexander Donovan is rich, good-looking, an eligible bachelor, and he's local...The man made his first million at age twenty-five, without the benefit of a college degree, and he hasn't looked back since...he would be a very good catch.'"

Metsy Hingle describes her successful hero differently in *Switched At The Altar*: "There was nothing nice or tame or polite about his kiss. It wasn't the kiss of a stuffed-shirt businessman whose life revolved around bottom lines and financial statements. It wasn't the kiss of a genius who held a string of degrees and equated love to a chemical reaction that could be monitored and controlled. It was the kiss of a ruthless warrior, a man who seized what he wanted. A man who would make love to a woman hard and fast, hot and thorough. A man who would demand everything from his partner and give everything of himself in return."

Although not every hero is wealthy, each hero exudes influence in whatever society he inhabits, and he is always rich in character. But I prefer the stories with a larger-than-life, powerful, affluent hero. Perhaps you've heard the expression: the bigger they are, the harder they fall (in love, that is)? The big hero makes for juicy stories. Let's face it, a rich man with character will forever be regarded as good husband material.

A man with charisma, self-confidence, sex appeal, humor, heart, and intelligence is a man who can have anything he wants out of life. Not surprisingly, he wants love, romance, fidelity, and trust. Now he's a hero.

Instead of doing all the wrong things, like the other woman does in romance books, learn from the heroine. Just be yourself, pursue what you believe in, work hard for what you want, keep your sense of humor, and when you come across a true hero, grab him. Many a working-class girl has seized the heart of a very successful man.

When I wrote my first book, I did not set out to write a romance. I wasn't even thinking of writing for publication. I wrote a story that intrigued me about characters I wanted to spend time with, get to know, find out what happened to them. I discovered myself in the process of writing that book. I found out what a romantic I am at heart. I'm an optimist. I believe that people are basically good and caring, and I celebrate the nobility of the human spirit by writing. Romance suits me well.

—Kathleen Eagle

7

Women in control of their lives are appealing to men in control of their lives

She might not be God's gift to Murano, but neither was she a little blonde tweet–tweet. She could work—she would work—she'd show them what English girls were made of.

—Liza Manning, The Glass Madonna

Romance novel heroines may not always start out in control of their lives, but they strive toward that outcome. A loss of control can be a traumatic, dreadful feeling. The more inner strength a person has, the more difficult to accept a loss of power.

But our heroine doesn't simply accept what life has dealt her. Rather, she fights to regain leverage. Her conviction gives her some semblance of control. This tenacity disarms the hero. Even if he disagrees with her, he can't help but admire her volition.

Sometimes our heroine may be in full control of her destiny before a twist of fate brings her head-to-head with the hero. She may be self-confident, independent, and creative. What kind of man might she meet and attract?

Ever notice how the woman who seems to have everything finds the most attractive, confident, successful man? Who hasn't heard of the captain of the football team hooking up with the head cheerleader? Now there's a pair of kindred spirits.

Just as we want the evil witch to hook up with someone who is equally nasty because they deserve each other, we want to see the fabulous heroine win that fantastic hero.

Today's heroine needs a man who is her equal. He must match her strength. In fact, the stronger and more self-reliant the woman, the stronger and more exceptional the man must be. Likewise, a dynamic hero wants a woman like himself. No, not masculine and brawny—a woman can be strong and still be feminine. He wants them to share similar mindsets.

Consider the opposite of our heroine—a woman who lacks confidence, wants a man to make all the decisions, who cowers when confronted and fails to stand up for herself or her beliefs. Would the same man fall for both our feisty heroine and her opposite? Probably not.

What kind of woman are you? What kind of men do you attract? Think about the type of mate you'd *like* to attract. Some women see a man they're attracted to and say, "He's out of my league. I could never have a man like that." Men think like that, too. Instead of limiting yourself to someone whom you perceive as being "in your league," evaluate the qualities truly important to you. Then don't settle for less. And keep in mind, that person has his own list of priorities that often mirror his own strengths (and weaknesses).

Everyone wants a considerate, smart, upbeat, sexy mate with a sense of humor. These are seductive traits. There's something appealing about a man in control of his life. You feel secure with him, relaxed. He'll take care of his family in good times and bad. But it works both ways. Men don't want women whose lives are a mess. Unpaid bills, lack of direction, and other signs of irresponsibility are not very romantic.

Before you hit the town with a wish list for a man, get control of your own life first. Take action. Concentrate your efforts on what matters most to you. *Be* the kind of person you want your mate to be. Strive for it.

Romance is a major ingredient of the glue that helps to hold a marriage or relationship together. Doing romantic things tells your beloved that you still find him/her desirable, no matter how long you've been together. It's made up of big things like love, respect, commitment, and surprises; it's also made up of little things, like a tender touch, a note left behind somewhere unusual on a small scrap of paper, help with a chore, a smile across a room, sitting and chatting or even being silent when no one else is around, or a hug/cuddle/kiss after a hard day at the office or with the children; and it's having fun together and finding your beloved funny. As for romance novels, they can teach valuable lessons about emotions and relationships; and they allow readers to share in the characters' lives and feelings, to watch a first attraction blossom into beautiful love forever.

—**Janelle Taylor**

True love is worth the risk

8

> *Loving Rob would only bring her sorrow. She couldn't,
> wouldn't spend the rest of her life being afraid for him,
> worrying every time he left that this time he might not
> come back. Tears of hopelessness, frustration, and disgust
> with herself for not being stronger slipped from beneath
> her lids...*
>
> **—Cynthia Van Rooy, A Man in Uniform**

In romance novels grown men who are hardened warriors, shrewd businessmen, tough cops, or otherwise intimidating adversaries view risk as part of a day's work. Danger is expected and handled. Death is often the price for failure. But these same invincible men will also bolt from a woman they could love. They hightail it without bothering to fill out a change-of-address form. Meaningful relationships elude them. Why?

Falling in love is the ultimate gamble. To risk one's heart and soul is terrifying. Love is unpredictable and uncontrollable. For men who demand full control, surrender may be too high a price. While these fearless men learned the laws of survival, they were never taught to put their heart in someone else's hands. No wonder they put up such a fight.

And put up a respectable fight they do. Only a self-assured woman has a chance; only a woman who absolutely believes in the man can teach him to open his heart. She must know, beyond doubt, that what's in her own heart is real.

In some cases, the man was hurt deeply. He vows never to risk commitment again. Establishing a relationship with him isn't effortless. With the right woman, his affection grows as his heart heals.

The woman also can be the one afraid to risk herself. In Cynthia Van Rooy's novel *A Man in Uniform*, the heroine pledges never to love a man with a dangerous job. In any of these examples, when one of the parties fears love, the other must become the pursuer, otherwise nothing will develop and the relationship will be over before it has a chance to start. One person must realize the gain is worth the risk. It makes no difference if the man or the woman takes the initiative, as long as one of them does. Through time and persistence, the other learns that love is the ultimate reward.

This breakthrough is one beauty of romance novels. When the person finally lets his or her guard down and finally trusts, it's a rare, heartfelt moment. We are thrilled for them both. They discover the anguish is worth the outcome.

Wild Heart by Jane Bonander features a hero who fears he is not good enough for the heroine: "'From the first moment I saw you, I knew you were a woman out of my reach. I thought to myself, *What could I do to deserve her?* I couldn't think of a damned thing. You were smart and witty. Noble and brave. And a whole passel of exciting contradictions I've only begun to understand.' The heroine replies, 'Do you know what you've done for me?... You've made me feel beautiful. You've brought passion and love into my life, and I never believed it would happen to me.'"

The hero and heroine in Sandra Brown's unforgettable novel *Breath of Scandal* both have painful pasts. For them, learning to love again is a monumental risk. It takes guts for them to truly face their ghosts and let go of past injustices, but they realize love is worth the anguish. And the pain is a little easier to bear when a loved one is standing by their side.

Nothing in life worth having is easy. Love has its ups and downs, its nonsense. Love takes time; it takes work. The risks are immense. Always remember, just because you won't let yourself fall in love doesn't guarantee you'll never be let down or hurt. Nor does it guarantee you'll be in full control of your life and emotions.

But, when in love the heart soars, expands, overflows. True love means a complete bonding of souls, an unceasing faith, respect, and trust in the individual and the relationship. True love is not a common occurrence, and it's not something to take for granted. Although one often must risk much to win true love, it is a hard-won gift meant to be treasured.

Romance novels are part of a worldwide sub-culture of women. They cross barriers of race, language, and class because at the heart they deal with the most momentous decision of a woman's life—choosing a mate she can trust enough to have his children. Around this central theme they treat contemporary issues of interest and importance to women—relationships—the dilemmas and crises women face every day when they are torn between their own needs and the needs of a loved one, whether parent, child, lover or friend. The books set out primarily to entertain, and that is why people read them, but along the way they sometimes find presented to them a problem that may arise in their own lives, and show how one fictional woman resolved it. No romance purports to give The Right Answer to the Meaning of Life, but some will help readers to frame the right questions.

—Daphne Clair de Jong

Communication is the key to a healthy relationship

9

> *"Animals have more sense than human beings,"*
> *he said softly...*
> *"We're not animals," she whispered. "We're*
> *people. Life isn't so simple for us..."*
> *For a long moment he looked away, across the*
> *meadow and forest and beyond to the distant*
> *mountains. "Sometimes things are simple,"*
> *he murmured.*
>
> **—Susan Krinard, Prince of Wolves**

Ever read a book where you wanted to strangle a character? You know the type of book I'm referring to, the kind where a simple conversation would clear everything in question. But for whatever reason, the character clams up, doesn't say the right words. The character believes he has a good reason to keep quiet, and the reason can be valid: blackmail, misinformation, shame, pride, protection of loved ones, to name a few. Other rationalizing to keep feelings to oneself just doesn't make sense. Of course in love and war, common sense isn't always a guarantee.

I'm not referring to people who really have done something terrible for which they need to apologize or seek redemption, nor to those attempting revenge. They have a motivation to keep their thoughts to themselves. I'm pointing out those characters who know a misunderstanding has taken place but they do nothing to absolve themselves. Or worse, by inaction, they allow the misunderstanding to deepen.

Think about it this way. If you had a chance to build a relationship with the one person you really loved and admired, would you let him think wrongly of you and lose him forever? If so, why? Isn't it better to face your fears, tell the truth, and let the chips fall where they may? What have you got to lose?

I'd rather lose by the truth than lose by a misunderstanding. Otherwise, you'll never know if having the courage to communicate and try to clear the air would have made a difference. By getting things out in the open, you clarify disagreements and stop negative feelings from increasing. Even if you argue, you affirm that the relationship can survive this bump and other problems in the future.

That's all there is to it—to avoid becoming one of those wimpy, unsympathetic characters, all you have to do is talk and listen. Say what's on your mind or in your heart. Then listen, genuinely listen, to what's being said. While you're at it, look for the nonverbal signs, too. Read his body language, the look on his face. Just ask a question. Spit it out. Squash those misunderstandings before they take root. And if, occasionally, you put your foot in your mouth, it won't be the end of the world. Just think before you speak.

Communicating doesn't mean 'name calling' or acting like a shrew. The heroine in a romance never stoops to that level. She never belittles or ridicules and neither does the hero. They may snip and snipe at one another, but never maliciously.

So, to all heroines out there: Heroes do not come equipped with ESP. They cannot read your thoughts. You must do some talking— and listening. This is called communication. Active communication is vital for a healthy relationship.

I learned that women are strong and that life doesn't have to be hopeless; after a lifetime of studying modernist literature, that was one hell of an epiphany.

—Jennifer Crusie

If you don't treat your partner right, someone else will

10

> *"I need a wife…"*
> *"What?"*
> *"You heard me. I'm gonna pick one of those gals,*
> *maybe the one who wants to hear about the great outdoors*
> *and pamper her man with home-cooked meals."*
> *"I see."*
> *"What's wrong? Why are you looking at me that way?"*
>
> **—Carol Grace, Wife For a Night**

There are three rules for writing a successful romance novel: Focus on the relationship. Focus on the relationship. Focus on the relationship. I think it's a great motto for marriage, too. With all the deadbeats out there, a good man will be snatched up by another woman before you have time to change the sheets. Good men truly are hard to find. I realized this after watching numerous friends and relatives having a difficult time with their significant others. Their complaints, though similar, went from, "poor personal hygiene," "uncultured," "unwilling to commit," "too picky," "not very considerate," and "not very interesting," to "doesn't help around the house," "can't keep a job," "doesn't know how to fix things," or "not an attentive lover."

Look at that list of complaints. If you're involved with a man who passes all these criteria, hold onto him.

Frequently, our hero has a woman in the wings who has taken him for granted, just doesn't appreciate what she has, or is more concerned in looking out for her own interests than for her man's. That's usually when our heroine walks onto the scene.

The heroine regrets that the remarkable man is taken, but she graciously backs off. A true romance novel heroine does not pursue a taken man. Naturally, circumstances will throw them into strained situations causing intense sexually charged conflict. However, the desire isn't acted upon—not until the man frees himself from the failed relationship with the other woman.

The other woman puts up a good battle, even if only to save face. She's formidable competition with her experience, beauty, special talents, and cunning mind. Sometimes she's considerably more sophisticated than the heroine. Other times she has a history with the hero and his family. But the message is clear: If she'd been treating him right to begin with, he never would have strayed. Never. Because a true romance novel hero does not womanize. This woman didn't treat her man with the appreciation, respect, and love he craved, so he unwittingly fell for someone who did.

Before the men out there start to gloat, they need to remember this applies to them, too. Sometimes the heroine is engaged to another man before the hero waltzes into the picture and steals her heart.

On the other hand, there are actually women out there who want to steal your man away from you. They are conniving and plotting at this moment. We've seen it, read about it, maybe experienced it; we know that it happens. Some women don't care if a man is taken. If they want him, they'll go after him.

Look at the way Joanne Pence shows women's scheming behavior in *Something's Cooking*: "Loretta stuck her head in the lounge, 'Your sexy friend is pacing around waiting for you. And about six women are closing in on him.' Without a word, Angie left, walked straight to Paavo, hooked her arm in his, and led him to the other side of the room."

Smart move by the heroine. So what can we do to protect our unsuspecting men from the clutches of these enticing predators? What do our heroines do?

They put their highest effort into what matters to them. This includes interactions with the hero. Almost nothing is done so-so. If there's one thing our books have in common no matter what subgenre, be it contemporary, historical, or suspense, it's hurling the hero and heroine together. They are always in touch. They are never more than a page away. The developing relationship becomes meaningful to them.

Let your mate know how important your relationship is to you. And consider another writing maxim: show, don't tell.

When I began writing romance, it was because I loved reading romances. The words came straight from my heart and when I discovered the power those words had in touching another person's heart, I was overwhelmed with joy in knowing that something I had done could make a difference in someone else's life. Romance novels tell a story, but more importantly they define a sisterhood.

—**Shirley Hailstock**

Whining
isn't attractive

11

> Desolation swept through her, but before
> tears could destroy her fragile composure,
> she climbed from the tub and briskly
> toweled herself dry. She must not allow
> herself to sink into melancholy, for
> she needed all her strength.

—**Mary Jo Putney, Mad, Bad, and Dangerous to Know**

Whining annihilates romantic interest faster than finding a mouse in your bed. If quelling intimacy isn't reason enough to stop, ponder this—whining is not a noble trait.

People don't appreciate listening to a whiner. And why should they? Everyone has problems. Why would individuals want to hear new ones, or be reminded of their own? People who whine come across as selfish, uncreative, spineless, and obtuse. Whining tells us a person can't handle a little unpleasantness like most of us can, or that a person isn't used to solving life's trivial problems. The self-centered whiner usually doesn't notice that no one else is complaining.

The way men and women react to whining is also revealing. Do they listen, ignore, groan, interrupt, or throttle the whiner? (The latter is what I'd like to do.) And imagine if everyone whined. How unproductive we'd all be—we'd whine and dine alone; we could wail watch off the coast; or be contestants on Squeal of Fortune. I'd no more whine that I'd snivel, grovel, cower, gripe, or nag, because it doesn't get you anywhere. As a rule, the whiner loses respect, dignity, time, and perspective.

In a book, such sniveling is no less annoying than it is in a person. I want the character to toughen up. Here's a simple illustration: A terrible catastrophe hits a town and families lose their homes. The whiner is upset that a party she carefully planned must be canceled. I'd like to say, "Look at what the heroine's been through. She doesn't feel sorry for herself."

One of my favorite stories is Margaret Mitchell's *Gone With the Wind*. Scarlett is a fine example of the strong heroine who does not whine. She forges ahead in the face of hardship. While her whole world is being torn apart by war, she has the will to survive, the courage to save her home and protect her family. Likewise for Rhett, whining isn't in his vocabulary. He's a self-assured, vigorous man. He's not one to let obstacles stand in his way. Scarlett and Rhett's admirable strength of character is what separates them from the norm and makes them riveting.

Whining is unromantic, unheroic, and downright useless. You'll never hear a heroine whine. She may protest or point out negatives, but her challenge gets results, inspires action. No matter the heavy load she carries, she perseveres. When life throws too much at her, she can cry and still be heroic. In moderation, crying doesn't make a man or woman weak; any amount of whining does.

As for the hero, you'll never hear a real man snivel. He may argue or be bullheaded, of course. His riled conduct gets his point across, persuades. A man could have everything going for him, but if he whines, no one, of either sex, will tolerate him for long. And although it's acceptable for a man to cry, to be so emotionally overcome that he breaks down, it's not manly to whine. No matter how down on his luck the hero is, he maintains his dignity. If you think you can't identify a real man, think again—the hero will hold your interest, while the whiner will turn you off.

I came late to romance novels. I discovered them at the PX when I was an army lieutenant. One sample, and I was hooked. I always had been a reader, but now I scoured the shelves, looking for more of these wonderful books, and, from that time, I never was without one or more romances. I remember when my children were small, having one child clinging to each leg as I made supper while I'd be stirring some sauce with one hand and holding a romance novel in the other. Romance novels were my guide to fabulous places and times that I could not get to with three small children and a large mortgage. When I began to write my own stories, it was still for that reason. I love historicals and Regencies, because they allow me to have my own time machine that can sweep me (and my readers) anywhere and any time. Writing these books allows me to fall in love for the first time over and over. What could be more wonderful?

—JoAnn Ferguson

Never trust anything a woman who has her eye on your man tells you

12

> She was all over John Cabot. Georgina's John Cabot... Phoebe Dearborn laughed like a braying goat with the hiccups, and whenever she was around a man she fluttered her eyelashes and cooed. It was common knowledge that Phoebe had more faces than the town clock.
>
> **—Jill Barnett, Carried Away**

There's a woman who has an interest in your man. You've seen her moisten her lips seductively, cross and uncross her legs alluringly in his presence, and otherwise flirt with him. She isn't one to stop at batting her eyelashes at him. Would you honestly trust this woman to tell you the truth about your man?

Could you in good conscience even leave your husband or boyfriend alone with her in the first place? I know, I know, we can't put a leash on our mates, and we are supposed to trust them all the time. But, somehow, this woman finds a way to corner him. She has her moment to tempt him with her charms. Then she has the opportunity to make up whatever story she wants to tell.

I like this kind of novel. They're about temptation, lies, jealousy, conniving, self-confidence, trust, and love. They're compelling books and the plots can go in any number of directions.

Sometimes, the one planting the seed of doubt is a relative, as in Emma Goldrick's *Thunder Over Eden*. "'What are you, another one of Rafe's live-in girlfriends?... You're not much like the other women Rafe has paraded through here. Did you know that?'"

Sometimes, the heroine actually believes this other woman. Maybe the evidence stacks up too high against the hero. Maybe it's because of some deep-rooted inferiority complex or that the vixen's story is so believable. Still, you'd think the heroine would question the other person's claims. But no, that would be too logical; she falls for the lies, distrusts the hero, and allows a fracture to widen between them.

The other woman has her moments soaking up her victory. That was so effortless, she surmises. The gullible heroine will be left with nothing but her troubled thoughts and empty memories.

Finally, something gives the heroine a kick in the pants. She grasps the notion she has to fight fire with fire. She sets out on a mission to win back her man, who, understandably, may be hesitant. After all, she didn't believe in him, so who's to say she wouldn't dump him again? Distrust is like lava pouring out of a volcano, as it destroys everything it encounters. Reading about it is much better than living it.

Though, sometimes, in spite of how much we trust someone, the evidence does incriminate him. How do we forestall evil forces from entering our lives? Here are suggestions derived from romance novel heroines who didn't swallow the deception but instead challenged the other woman's claims head-on.

First, look at the motives of the person who casually mentions unpleasant "facts" about your partner. Ask yourself, what does she have to gain? Why is she telling you this; is it to inform, hurt, or warn? What does she think you should do about it; leave him, argue, or say nothing and let it gnaw at your insides? Second, ignore the messenger's advice and follow your own instincts. Third, look at the situation from all sides, particularly your mate's. Maybe the hussy exaggerated. Fourth, know in your heart that your husband or boyfriend isn't capable of the actions she has described and confirm it the minute you see him. Or, confirm it yourself, inherently, without ever having to ask. Now, that's trust. That kind of confidence in your man will send the other woman running away with her tail between her legs. She can't fight your strength, your unfailing love.

The other woman can't win when the heroine's actions are noble. If you're in doubt about your partner, think about this: It's the heroine's actions that have the greatest impact on who wins and who loses.

When I read a romance novel, I can forget about everything that needs to be done and lose myself in a world where love prevails no matter what the obstacles and happily-ever-after endings are guaranteed.

—Melissa Martinez McClone

You can make up 13
for lack of experience
with enthusiasm

> *There was a powerful urgency in him that*
> *roused me to response despite his awkwardness...*
> *As yet too hungry and too clumsy for tenderness,*
> *still he made love with a sort of unflagging joy*
> *that made me think that male virginity might*
> *be a highly underrated commodity.*

—Diana Gabaldon, Outlander

Experience with a lack of fervor, or inexperience with spirited enthusiasm; which would you prefer? The romance novel hero, time and time again, selects the lady with the can-do attitude. We're not just talking sex here, but every aspect of the heroine's life. Why? Put yourself in his position. A person with enthusiasm is willing to learn, try new things, and is eager to please.

Wait a minute, you say. The romance heroine isn't so congenial or passive. She's her own woman, stands up for herself, goes after what she wants. You're absolutely right. Her enthusiasm comes naturally from the heart. Her efforts mean something important to her. When the stakes are vital, she pours herself into the venture. Her love, longing, belief, and excitement for the task at hand causes her to respond quite passionately.

Romance novel heroines have nursed the sick back to health, raised children alone, taken up a rifle to defend the family's land, trudged along treacherous frontier trails, or led crusades. Often, the heroine hasn't received formal training. Her reactions are spontaneous. She's not worrying about her shyness, ineptness, or lack of experience. At the intuitive level, gut instincts guide the way. The heroine does what she must, what she's compelled to do.

These points hold true for intimate situations as well. A great example is in Rebecca Winter's *Second-Best Wife*: "Gaby had so little experience with men, she had no idea what she was doing. Right now she was driven by sheer, primitive female instinct. The man she wanted was about to disappear from her life, never to be seen again. Until he thrust her away from him, she would show him just exactly what he meant to her."

On the other hand, not all heroines are complete novices. Many are bright, educated, and know exactly what they're doing. Sometimes, as in the scene from Diana Gabaldon's book *Outlander*, it works the other way around—the woman is the one with the sexual expertise.

If an inexperienced heroine meets an experienced male, how does she measure up to his sophistication and worldliness? Mostly, our heroine is not concerned about him at all. She's too busy living life and facing its complications to worry about romance.

Besides, nowadays more heroines are worldly themselves: an old hat at one thing, a newcomer at something else. It's the way she tackles the unknown that makes her admirable. Our heroine braves the risk of humiliation, defeat, or death when she's out of her element. No wonder she busts her butt. Though your choices may not be that detrimental or extreme, apply yourself as if they were and see what happens.

Sometimes society prefers beginners. That's why we have apprentices, recruits, and training programs. Consider that amateurs may be more free-spirited, more gutsy, and less lackadaisical. Bottom line, they haven't 'been there, done that.'

Does your enthusiasm for what you love show? If not, here's what to do: Don't hold back. Let your enthusiasm shine. Don't be afraid. Open your heart. Follow your passions, not for a man, but for yourself. You'll live life more completely and find it more satisfying.

As many of our heroines have discovered, you may decide being a novice isn't so bad. And, you may find that other people notice and applaud your enthusiastic approach to life.

A romance novel is one of the few things we, as readers, can count on to provide a little ray of sunshine in an often dreary world. By reading romances, I come away feeling better about life in general.

—**Rosalyn Alsobrook**

Your past will always catch up with you

14

> But she had never understood until that moment,
> until she looked down into his face, why the eyes
> were called windows into the soul. In the gloomy
> light his eyes glittered up at her, fierce and wild,
> and haunted with old and terrible fears.

—Penelope Williamson, The Outsider

Heroines are no stranger to the running and hiding department. Mostly their pasts are dreadful, and we don't blame them for starting over. Romance novels are replete with strong women who take the initiative to start a new life. That's commendable. Whenever I think of the different histories of romance novel heroines, I'm grateful I lead a bland, normal life in comparison.

Why try to flee the past? Wanting a better future, avoiding humiliation, escaping the law, and fear. The consequences of facing a predicament are unbearable. Starting over becomes the best option. There's nothing wrong with that.

Rebuilding is good. Often, it's a matter of moving on; at other times it requires an elaborate scheme that includes keeping a secret or running away. Frequently, the heroine makes the right choice in running, but sometimes she's regretful. There's no guarantee of favorable end results.

Even hiding out for a short hiatus to regroup can lead to deceptive measures. Concealment becomes a white lie that grows and grows. Not only in novels, but in life, if one tells too many lies, keeping track of them becomes difficult and creates new problems. Also, there's a loss of intimacy when there's a significant secret between two people. Honesty in a relationship is important. Certainly one doesn't need to tell everything to a spouse, but a precarious lie, kept hidden, may surface when least expected.

It's not the small cover-ups that ruin lives—the big misrepresentations do the most damage. Not that she's hiding a past life as a vampire, but that she was betrothed to a despicable enemy. Maybe she'd been married before, and her divorce from an absolute worm was never finalized. Nevertheless, a heroine believes she can rise above her former deeds and live a good life.

Ultimately the past catches up with her. When the past converges with the present, unwelcome complications develop, threatening the future. In other words, all hell breaks loose. The character is forced to confront the dilemma. Heroines, however apprehensive, deal with their problems because they know those problems will keep coming back to haunt them if they don't.

Tara Taylor Quinn's heroine in *Yesterday's Secrets* has everything to lose if her past is discovered. "Shannon's heart went numb with dread as the sheriff continued with his recitation of her rights. She had heard them all once before, twelve years ago, and her tired brain could hardly comprehend that it was happening again. After all these years, the efforts and disappointments, the pain and the humiliation, was she right back where she had started?"

As with a romance novel heroine, you may have good cause to leave your past behind, but it never fails; the past finds us. Sooner or later, those skeletons start to rattle. The impact on our lives depends on how equipped we are to deal with it and how honest we are with the people closest to us. It takes great courage to face a dark past. But sometimes that's the only way to break through to a promising future.

I write romance for the same reason I've read romance for years: I love the genre. I love losing myself in the challenges and trials of two characters who are destined to be together. I guess I want to believe that there's somebody for everyone, and that under just the right circumstances and with a bit of that magic we call romance, happily-ever-afters are within our reach.

Before you scoff and call me a Pollyanna, I assure you I'm enough in tune with reality to lock my doors and warn my children of strangers. I watch the news and I see the state of our world. But what do we have if we don't have hope? Romance is all about hope.

After my fourth book, Saint or Sinner, was released, I received the most memorable letter I've ever received from a reader. She told me how much she'd enjoyed my book, how she identified with the characters and how she'd cried for the heroine. Like the character in my story, she'd been stalked and beaten by someone who should have loved her. Unlike my character, however, the reader has permanent nerve damage to her arm. Her story touched me so deeply that it brought tears to my eyes and gave me pause to think over what I was doing.

I sat at my desk thinking how shallow my work is. I make all this stuff up! I order peoples' lives about and manipulate them to suit my plots, but it's all fiction. And then I realized why this young woman had been touched so profoundly by my story. She said she hoped that some day she would meet a man like Joshua, a man who would love her. She had hope. Romance is about hope.

We invest our time in the characters in these stories because we know that no matter what dilemmas befall them, no matter which conflicts arise, in the end, love will conquer all; good will win over evil; and a happily-ever-after will prevail.

Each of us hopes there is that special someone out there, the man or woman who will love us and fill that place created in our heart just for them. Romance brings that hope to life, and through the stories of love and commitment, we experience the fulfillment of the human dream.

—**Cheryl St. John**

If you stand around waiting for a man, you'll be alone a long time

15

> Rose, who had planned to laugh in a flirty,
> sophisticated way, managed one squeak and
> gave up... She'd made it this far. Her plan
> was working. She'd wangled a lunch invitation
> from him. She was going to talk with him.
> She was going to fascinate him. She was going
> to throw up.
>
> **—Heather Allison, His Cinderella Bride**

Though the heroine's goal at the beginning of the book has nothing to do with getting an "MRS." degree, there are times when a heroine knows she wants a man, and she makes a plan to get that man. A woman-pursuing-man story is delightful as well as educational. The woman plots out intricate ways to be near the hero. She gets hired by his company, she knows when he's expected at a certain place and happens to be there, or she gets herself noticed through her distinctive talents.

Once she has his attention, it's up to her to keep it. And she won't keep it for long if she hasn't been herself or if she doesn't have her own unique appeal.

Certainly, as in the case of Heather Allison's *His Cinderella Bride*, the heroine can have her heart set on a special man. But she doesn't wait around for him to somehow discover that she's the woman of his dreams. Rather, she takes the situation into her own hands. Even if she's a bit green, she has daring.

Yet however much she wants him, she's a woman with her own life, her own individual aspirations and interests. Not once, in all the twenty-something years I've been reading romance novels, has the heroine said, "I need a man to feel worthy" or "I won't be happy until I get myself a man." Not once. The heroine of the novel is not waiting until she nabs a man for her life to start. She lives her life in the here and now—and she has things to do, places to go, and people to see. She does not define her worth by the men she attracts. (This concept is not contradictory to the heroine seeking a marriage of convenience. Such an agreement is used to solve a problem. It's not an arrangement to make the heroine feel complete or give her life more meaning. We'll revisit this later in Chapter 21.)

Think about the men you've been drawn to. Were you attracted to the guy who had no ambition, no specialties, nothing that excited him? Or was he a guy who buried himself in his career, hobby, or political cause?

I always admired the guy with a passion for something—the one with his fascination for baseball, playing the trumpet, UFOs, or learning Italian, and the one with a dream to improve himself in that preoccupation of his. I can't recall ever being attracted to a man who only wanted to find a woman to make his life complete. That thought is creepy, to say the least.

Besides, having a man doesn't mean your life will suddenly be care-free. You're still the same person, with all the baggage, skills, and habits you had before.

Instead of waiting for a man or anything else, live now. Have fun. Don't let life pass you by. I'm not suggesting you follow the '60s mentality of 'live for today' but instead am saying that being happy doesn't have to include a white wedding with all the trimmings, even if that's what you ultimately want. Happiness could mean taking that night class in Japanese cooking, earning a college degree, or becoming a godparent to your best friend's daughter.

Cultivate your interests and make your own path. And learn from heroines: You'll never get anywhere by merely wishing and dreaming. You've got to carry out your plans. If those plans include pursuing a special man, all the power to you. Along the way, find the joys in your daily world. You have the ingredients within to satisfy yourself.

A confirmed optimist, I believe that, to a certain extent, we create our own environment. Today's romances are about today's women facing today's problems. They deal with a variety of issues with a great deal of common sense and an attitude of hopefulness that I believe is important. Why do I write romances? Because I love them. Because nobody ever told me I couldn't. Because words evoke images, and images create new worlds, and I want to explore as many of those worlds as possible, and take along as many readers as I can.

—Dixie Browning

Attitude makes all the difference

16

"It doesn't matter how much money you have," he drawled. "If you have your sights set on a fashionable marriage you'll need to improve your grammar, diction, manners, and almost everything else... "
"I just don't understand this laidy business." She bit her lip...
"Of course there are advantages to being a lady."
She raised her chin. "Like whot?"
"When you speak and act properly people will treat you with more respect."
She met his bemused gaze without flinching. "They treats me with respect now or I'll give 'em a pastin' they'll never forget!"

—Sonya Birmingham, Almost a Lady

No matter how wealthy you are, how educated or how stylishly you dress, if you have a bad attitude, no one will care. A successful person doesn't need to flaunt her successes or prosperity to gain notice. Her individuality attracts the right attention.

In a romance novel, we can tell who the players are by their attitudes. We know who the friends are and of whom we should be wary. We know the snobs and the kindhearted. We know who is right for whom. Ever read a book with an uppity, impatient, or selfish woman who behaves sweetly around the hero? Although she may also be accomplished and smart, we know this woman's

77

nasty temperament won't work with the hero's personality, and we can't wait for him to discover this fact.

While story characters may wear their hearts on their sleeves, in reality, seeing beneath a person's facade may not be so easy. But, like an author's carefully planted clues, a person's true colors will eventually unfold. We demonstrate our attitudes in our actions, dialogues, and habits just as in the novels.

If we follow the example set by our romance novel heroine, we too can redeem ourselves after making mistakes. She has a great attitude toward life. She accepts her attributes and shortcomings if she has no control over them. Our heroine works with what she has, and her most important asset is her attitude. Her motto: It's not your position in society that's important, it's your attitude that counts. Even if wrongly assessed by people, her spirit isn't dampened. With a confident, upbeat, candid attitude there is nothing that can keep her back.

Our attitude affects our decisions and our lives, how others perceive us and react to us. Our disposition can make us ugly or beautiful. Attitude is the thing that can get us into trouble or pull us out of trouble. It influences our happiness.

Margaret Brownley eloquently proves this point in her novel *Touch of Lace*: "'Because of you, I was forced to see myself without the scar. It was a frightening moment because with it came the realization that I wasn't crippled or deformed, I was a normal person who just happened to have a scar.' 'Everyone has scars,' Abby said. 'Some of them are inside and I'm afraid those are the hardest to hide. You can't put powder or cream on those.'"

Well said. We all do have scars, but our attitude about them is what people really see.

Attitude influences everything. The right attitude at the right time makes all the difference in the world. Do you need an attitude adjustment, or is your attitude winning you friends and overcoming your enemies?

I enjoy reading romances for their feel-good, happy endings. For me, it's a reaffirmation that men and women, despite seemingly insurmountable obstacles, can find the strength and the courage within themselves to overcome whatever life tosses their way. I enjoy seeing the empowerment of women as the book evolves, and watching the men who love them struggle with their own emotions. My enjoyment has increased now that African-American romances are available to show more of America's rich cultural diversity. After all, just like in life, character, not skin color, shows a person's true worth.

—**Francis Ray**

Real heroes do not wear suits of armor these days

...she couldn't help but wonder what kind of a woman would have put her marriage to Jonah in jeopardy. Sarah surmised that his wife had to have been mentally unstable to risk losing anyone as remarkable. It didn't make sense. Sarah couldn't think of another person who came close to being his equal. No man of her acquaintance compared to him in any way, shape or form.

—Rebecca Winters, Return to Sender

Women everywhere ask, "Where have all the real men gone? Have the feminists chased them away?" They miss being treated to the courtesies of a man opening a door, pulling out a chair, not cursing in her presence—the old-fashioned stuff. Some want not only the common indulgences but a man who won't mind if she choses to stay home and raise their family while he earns the money. Women want men who will treat them with courtesy and respect. These men are still around, but, because of changing times, they're now often camouflaged. But don't despair, chivalry is alive and well.

While today's real man doesn't ride atop a horse in a suit of armor, nor fight off fire-breathing dragons, he is brave nonetheless. He turned in his suit of armor and lance for a business suit and briefcase, or utility belt and hard-hat, or a badge and gun. He faces a different kind of dragon. In his contemporary lifestyle he deals with a global perspective; the price of tea in China just might affect him. It's a fast-paced, unpredictable, dog-eat-dog world.

Yet, we still have gallant, romantic men who remember to bring home roses and a bottle of wine once in a while. They might not pick their clothes up off the floor, but they protect their loved ones from the outside harshness. Although it would be easier to walk away from their commitments, they stick around, providing security for their family. There's nothing more rousing than men who say, "Divorce isn't an option." They're in it for the long haul.

A typical man dreams about whisking away his mate for a romantic interlude, but there's not much free time for this. After all, a knight in shining armor didn't have a 50-hour-a-week job; didn't have a kid needing a ride to a soccer game, help with his homework or batting practice, or discipline to finish chores. In other words, today's hero has real responsibilities (and lots of them).

He might not be as courteous as his gentlemanly predecessor of yesteryear, but at least he's not as barbaric as a smelly old medieval knight either. Let's not kid ourselves, being married to a knight probably wasn't all it was cracked up to be. Could you imagine doing his laundry? Besides I'm sure that knight came home cranky from work, too. Who wouldn't after living in that ghastly metal suit for a month? And who do you think had to prepare the food for all those feasts, not to mention cleaning up afterward? Talk about a damsel in distress!

Real men are everywhere. You can't look only for the fancy, shiny armor. Instead of concentrating on bulging muscles, designer suits, expensive cars, or posh apartments, look for the important qualities of real men.

A real man works hard, plays hard, laughs deeply, pays bills, votes, cares about his loved ones, appreciates and respects his woman. He has intestinal fortitude, determination, and foresight. He is the guy who quietly, day in and day out, helps to keep the country going. A real man isn't a liar or a coward, nor is he envious, vain, untrustworthy, or cruel.

Some guys aren't the brightest but they have lots of character. These men aren't flawless, they've made mistakes. They can be exasperating. But we don't give up on them, and we love them just the way they are.

So remember that real men do exist outside the pages of a romance novel. He won't be wearing shining armor, and his intangible shield may be a bit chipped, but underneath, he's a real man. He's probably wearing shabby jeans and a torn T-shirt. There's a chivalrous man out there for you, too. When you find him, be kind, because more than likely, he's had a long day—just like you! Nurture his chivalrous spirit, and it will pay off in the long run.

Throughout time, we have sought romantic love. It is the common denominator of humanity and transcends gender, race, creed, and nationality. Romance novels reveal the dreams of the heart, the hopes of the spirit, and the lengths we're willing to go to find love—even across time itself. Pick up a romance novel and you've picked up a book of hope with a happy ending. We need more hope, more dreams, and more smiles.

—Susan Plunkett

Real heroines look for the opportunities in their situation

18

> Thea stared at her. "But he has a gun."
> "Oh pooh! That little toy? I've shot
> better guns than that," Evadne said,
> making Thea look at her with new respect.
> "We'll have to distract him somehow.
> He's only a man. Surely we can outwit him."
>
> —**Mary Kingsley, An Intriguing Affair**

Like ordinary women, romance novel heroines have faced life's most severe challenges. They've had to face loss, scandal, injustice, loneliness, illness, and financial ruin. How each woman approaches these difficulties is as varied as the woman herself. Women may be the most resilient creatures on the planet. I admire women who keep believing they can make a go of it, and exert themselves to defeat the negative influences trying to pull them down. Having faith isn't easy these days, but it's necessary, now more than ever in this crazy, mixed-up world.

Overcoming challenges is almost impossible without hope. I think that's one of the greatest gifts of romance novels—they offer readers hope.

Romances give hope that guts, resolve, and hard work will pay off;

hope that trusting in one's beliefs and values while taking matters into one's own hands will lead a person in the right direction. But the greatest hope that romance novels give is the faith that love conquers all and will guide the way.

With that kind of confidence within her, a heroine will succeed. A heroine seeks and finds opportunities to turn things around to her advantage. It's her power of love that reinforces her. That's the one ingredient that makes her invincible.

When I read a book with a courageous heroine who overcame the odds, who stayed strong in the worst of circumstances, it rubs off on me. I want to be as brave and smart as she is. I'm encouraged that my faith in love, and in myself, will be strong enough to see me through any crisis.

Not all romances are so serious. Some are all-out hilarious, where the heroine's humor lightens the mood of an otherwise uptight situation. Susan Elizabeth Phillips does this superbly in *Nobody's Baby But Mine*, where, for valid reasons, the brainy heroine takes desperate measures to get pregnant by a dumb man. Her antics to entice the hero into bed are hilarious—and she learns that he's not as dumb as she thought. Jill Barnett's witticism in *Bewitching* is priceless. The heroine, an endearing witch, is not a typical sorceress. Her fumbling magic spells cause chaos and dismay. And Karen Robards takes a somber suspense plot and weaves in some of the most comical scenes I've ever read in her thriller *Walking After Midnight*. The heroine's fear of being chased by zombies turns out not to be unfounded—she faces very real danger—and she uses humor to keep from losing her wits while facing the bizarre situations she finds herself in.

Like an *Indiana Jones* movie where the hero takes a licking but keeps on kicking, a romance novel heroine has that kind of *chutzpah*. She's clever, strong, bold, and resourceful. Even when the chips are down, she doesn't let bad luck, bad karma, or a bad hair day get the best of her. Our heroine doesn't just look for the light at the end of the tunnel, but creates light 'inside' the tunnel as well. Her wit may save her as much as her endurance.

It's with these instruments that she rebels against her obstacles. She takes life one day at a time. Heroines are the kind of women we'd all like as best friends or sisters. They are people we can look up to, ask advice from, confide in, or get into mischief with. Someone to share the laughs or the tears. Who better to share with than another heroine? Because everyday women are the true heroines.

So when you're feeling down in the dumps, pick up a romance novel. You'll find inspiration, ideas, humor, and, most of all, hope. Through your personal efforts, you can make opportunities, too.

If I had a nickel for every time a fan has told me that reading a historical romance is the most painless way she knows to learn history, I'd be debt free for life. I must add, however, that as an erstwhile history teacher, I find _writing_ historicals to be the most painless—not to mention the most fun—way to teach history. Of course, the unspoken promise the author makes to the reader is to provide an accurate historical background _and_ a wonderful story. When the two meld successfully, what reader wouldn't prefer a history lesson that's woven into a tale full of action-packed adventure, laughter, tears, nerve-tingling romance, and perhaps even a mystery or two, all of which concludes with a satisfactory ending? If our schoolbooks were half as much fun to read, just imagine what the result might be!

—Amanda Scott

Emotions are timeless

19

> *1810 London*
> *"Lady Ann assures me that the earl is kind,*
> *not that I don't know that for myself, but*
> *people are strange, don't you think? Who can*
> *ever really know another person? What is in*
> *their hearts? In their thoughts? But don't*
> *worry Arabella, he is certain to be kind. If*
> *he is not, why then, you can simply shoot him."*
>
> **—Catherine Coulter, The Heir**

Before I read romance novels, I never thought I'd enjoy historical fiction or novels set in far off parts of the world. I summed it up like this: I can't identify with the characters. But I learned that human emotions do not go out of date. Stories about women and men beating the odds, good prevailing over evil, and people with strength of character and spirit coming out on top will always be timely.

Historical romance novels are about people first. These people have hopes, fears, dreams, and nightmares. They love and hate, feel envy, joy, and heartache. Like us, they have needs for acceptance, belonging, security, and self-esteem. Women in Regency romances and Civil War romances wanted these things as much as we do now. So even though the lifestyles, food, clothing, language, and expectations of women in 1600s Ireland, 1700s America, or 1800s England were distinct from each other and from those of modern-day women, on the inside we haven't changed all that much. We all would die to protect our families, yearn to be desired and loved, and want to live a content life. I imagine our predecessor sisters also wished for world peace, regardless of how large or small their world was.

There were trailblazing women in every era, women who sought out adventure, who pressed the boundaries of what was acceptable in their times. They guided warlike efforts or initiated campaigns for worthwhile causes. There were also wise homemakers and strong farmers who cultivated families as well as crops. These are the substance historical romances are made of. Combined with a difficult man, primal attraction, external and internal obstacles— now we have an interesting story.

The heart of the story we want to read is the romance. We might not otherwise pick up a book about cattle drives or about Viking warriors. But blend in a strong woman, overpowering motives, and colliding emotions and we're hooked, because we want to read about people falling in love. Love is as timeless as the stars. Whatever period in history, it is the glue that holds us together as a species. Technology might revolutionize, the planet and universe might evolve, but the human heart will stay the same. It can inflate with pride, gush with love, or be broken to bits.

In a romance novel, we read the stories of other women, from another time, and we feel a sense of togetherness. Through our universal emotions, we can empathize, experience the pleasures and sorrows of the characters, and learn about the time and place as if we were there ourselves.

A time-travel historical romance has a unique appeal. The traveler goes to a time where everything is unfamiliar. How can she possibly fall in love with a man raised in a foreign environment? The answer is revealed in three excellent time travel novels.

In Diana Gabaldon's *Outlander*, the heroine is comforted by a 1743 Scotsman. "[He] sat rocking me gently, muttering soft Gaelic in my ear and smoothing my hair...I wept bitterly...Jamie stroked my neck and back, offering me the comfort of his broad, warm chest. No wonder he was so good with horses, I thought blearily, feeling his fingers rubbing gently behind my ears, listening to the soothing, incomprehensible speech. If I were a horse, I'd let him ride me anywhere."

The heroine in Miriam Raftery's *Apollo's Fault* views her situation another way. "Still, even if he did have feelings for me, I could hardly chuck it all to stay in an era when women's thoughts were considered less important than the feathers in their hats. Could I?"

And Jude Deveraux's spellbinding novel *A Knight In Shining Armor* makes one positively believe time-defying love can happen. We see how love can make a person sacrifice everything and leap 400 years through time to save a soul mate.

We come to a conclusion we already knew: From 1743 to 1906 to 1998, and every year in between, women and men have had fundamental needs. For love, we'd go to the ends of the earth or consider staying in another place.

No matter the time period, love makes life worth living. Love ties are what separate humans from the rest of nature; they cause the most conflict and make for wonderful stories. For better or worse, much of history has been made from the most powerful of all emotions—love.

Love has always made the world go round. Romance novels capture that essence and make the spin all the sweeter.

My work ethic, my values and beliefs as a wife, mother, and woman in my own right are there for my family in person <u>and</u> in my books. In my stories, older, more traditional roles for girls such as teachers, waitresses, or receptionists have made room for jet pilots, trauma nurses, and forensic scientists. This must happen in real life as well if all our citizens, especially women, are to ever achieve their full potential. Children are our greatest resource, and the young women of today are the most neglected. My work as a writer has allowed me to do for my children and my readers—especially women readers—what I do for my fictional characters. I give them every opportunity to think, to change, to grow in new ways, all within a framework based on truth, love, family, and life-long !oyalty between one man and one woman. Every goal must start with a dream. If I spark one dream in one reader with my character's dreams...that's my reward with each and every book I write.

—Anne Marie Duquette

20

Just when you've convinced yourself you don't need a man, one comes along to change your mind

> "If he had looked at me the way he looked at you,
> I'd have melted on the spot."
> "Melting's not part of the job description, Karen."
> "No." Dreamy eyed, Karen put her hand on a ringing
> phone. "But it sure is part of being a woman..."
> If she'd been looking for a man, he would have fit
> the bill nicely. Opening up the phone book, Amanda
> reminded herself she was looking for a fax machine,
> not a man.

—Nora Roberts, A Man For Amanda

A romance novel heroine doesn't need a man in her life; she's strong enough to stand on her own, clever enough to make her own way. We first encounter many a heroine zipping along, minding her own business, happy, in control; when, all of a sudden, a man comes on the scene to ruin everything. Even when things are going all wrong for her, she doesn't need a man to solve her problems. Somehow, she will manage.

Why then do critics of romance novels think the heroine is a whimpering, helpless dimwit looking for a man to rescue her? The obvious answer is that since she does find a man by the end of the story, nonreaders believe that was her goal to start with. But we know the truth.

We know many a heroine has fought her attraction to the hero tooth and nail. We know she's discouraged him, threatened him, maybe even tried to defeat him. In many novels, the last thing the heroine wants is involvement with an exacerbating, interfering, sexy man.

The skeptics don't know what fun they're missing. It's entertaining to watch two independent, strong-willed people clash, not only with the other person, but within themselves. The repartee jumps off the page as these two maneuver for the upper hand. Their cool, logical protestations contradict the heated blood coursing through their veins—not as a result of anger, but due to desire.

An invisible force draws them together at the same time they mentally push themselves away. They deny they've met their match. They don't want to want another person. They like themselves the way they are—unattached.

Maybe our hero and heroine are so convinced they don't need a significant other that they forget that it's okay to want another person. Wanting is not a shortcoming but a basic human trait. When they give in to that desire, more friction arises because they haven't acknowledged that trait in themselves. They fear losing independence. For unyielding individuals, self-discovery is a long road. Once they get past their internal strife they can concede they indeed love each other, and therefore need each other.

Eventually, through anguish and imminent acceptance, they learn love doesn't weaken; love strengthens them. We know they are capable of making it alone, but they choose to face the world together. And when these two independent people unite, it makes a tender, inspiring story.

Good things do happen when you least expect them. You'll know a good thing when you see one. And remember, just because you didn't need him, doesn't mean you can't want him—like our resolute heroine, you can change your mind about needing a man, too. It's a woman's prerogative.

As the hero and heroine in Nora Roberts' *A Man For Amanda*, you, too, may realize, "Love shouldn't be smothered, or brushed carelessly away. It should be cherished..." even if it was the last thing you expected.

Romance novels are important. They've reinforced my awareness that mating bonds are the framework of human society. That such bonds are interesting—worthy even of literature without tragic endings. That a woman can be the central character of a novel, the one who makes things happen; just as women have always made things happen in the real world. And that good men know all this.

—Jo Beverley

Marriages of 21
convenience can work

> *"Marriage of convenience?"*
> *Annie leaned farther forward, intent on making*
> *him understand the brilliance of her plan. "By*
> *definition it's a marriage designed to benefit*
> *both parties in some manner but one that has*
> *nothing to do with love and affection. A*
> *marriage of convenience is essentially a*
> *business relationship..."*
> *"Annie, are you by any chance proposing to me?"*
>
> **—Jayne Ann Krentz, Wildest Hearts**

An act of desperation or suitable rationalization? A man and woman enter a marriage-of-convenience arrangement when one or the other decides that the image of marriage will solve all their problems. Marriage solve problems? Poor, naive souls. Many of us believe marriage is the cause of problems.

What do the hero and heroine usually think they're getting? A beneficial legal bond in name only. But in order for the marriage to be considered the real thing, the couple has to put up a public display of love and devotion. That means living together, being affectionate in public, going out on dates, and showing concern for each other's needs. Wait a minute, you say, I know people married for twenty years who never behave that way.

After the heroine digests unanticipated details of how the hero expects to enjoy the marriage, she feels sincere panic. The living arrangements cause the biggest challenge. The two are thrown together in intimate circumstances where they bump into one another in the hallway half naked. She catches a peek of him in the shower. He sees her in a skimpy nightie.

Then they have to act in love for the public. When discerning eyes are on the couple, the hero seizes the heroine in an unexpected soul-stirring kiss. Or the heroine will pull him close and whisper "Make it look believable" before branding him with a kiss that tightens his loins. But the kiss isn't really to satisfy the onlookers, it's to satisfy the sexual tension that's been building. It's not like they can run away to collect their thoughts—this person is going home with them every night.

Forced intimacy between two normally functioning, red-blooded, sexually deprived human beings who are married? They don't stand a chance. It doesn't make a difference if they make love or they resist the temptation because sex wasn't part of the bargain. Whatever choice they make only digs them in deeper, only makes them want the other person more. Inadvertently, they find themselves falling in love.

Serious feelings only add to their frustration. The hero rants and raves about petty things that have nothing to do with his actual problems. The heroine, denying she has affection for him, may pick fights to keep the distance between them.

But there are other things one notices when in the same house—thoughtfulness to others, good cooking, and creative problem-solving, to name a few. Keep in mind, in this relationship the hero and heroine have entered into the commitment without the traditional expectations of marriage. Neither expects the other person to be perfect. Each can be him- or herself without the typical anxiety caused by trying to impress the new spouse. Falling in love was unforseen.

This is when the ground falls out from under them and their new love is tested. It's an opportunity for one of them to back out, to admit he or she made a mistake. But our heroine comes to understand that she wasn't faking it at all. Her plea to him to "make it believable" was for her own visceral needs.

How do these marriages survive? The marriage may have started out as a convenience, but the act of desperation was also motivated by feelings the partners are not willing to acknowledge. That the ideal mate was selected for the temporary job signifies there was an attraction all along. Meanwhile, they've found captivating virtues in each other. They have watched each other closely; they have gotten to know each other. When their marriage is tested, both parties realize what the marriage means to them and confess that they want it to be real.

What can be learned from these potent stories? Even if you've been married for twenty years, you can make your marriage real, too. Don't expect your spouse to be perfect. Assure him, when your marriage is tested, that you want to make it work. Understand that sometimes arguments are caused by frustrations that have nothing to do with what is being said. Trying to behave in love in private might be more convincing, but take advantage of forced intimacy in your marriage, too.

The best love stories are fantasies in which the deep emotional values of love, family, and partnership in marriage emerge victorious over lesser values. Even when the ending is unhappy, the value of love triumphs. Hero and heroine are deeply altered by their love. They emerge from their struggles more emotionally whole than they began.

—Vanessa Grant, From her book Writing Romance

Trust your instincts 22

He knew something was wrong with Tina, knew it
gut deep, the way a bird knows to fly south, the
way a whale knows to migrate to its mating grounds.

—Laurie Paige, A River to Cross

Some naysayers of romance novels complain that coincidences fill
our books. They're convinced the stories are unbelievable, so the
fact that real life also contains dubious tales doesn't stop their
scorn.

On the surface, romance novel plots may seem coincidental or con-
trived, but a closer look reveals how important instincts can be.
Mother Nature provided humans and animals with built-in radar.
This quality of perception can serve as a warning system to alert us
to hazards. Or we might experience an enigmatic, but very tangible,
link with a person. These intrinsic reactions about situations or
people are a basic part of building a romance relationship.

What we feel for a person deep down may be tested by what we see
of the person before our eyes. But we have to remember that what
our innate senses tell us probably is correct. Gut instincts have

saved many a romance novel hero and heroine from tragedy. But survival depends on more than having a sense, it also relies on trusting one's intuition.

Often, learning to trust your own instincts is as difficult as learning to trust someone else. It does you no good to have a premonition if you ignore it. How many times have you heard someone say, "I knew better?" or "Why didn't I follow my hunch?"

Following our instincts when we have nothing else to go on can be frightening, but our heroes and heroines take that chance because they are not ones to sit and do nothing. When their instincts are correct, it is not a coincidence or contrivance.

Let's clarify some things contained in romance novels: Love at first sight isn't a contrivance, it happens all the time. It's fate, it's animal attraction, it's chemistry. A spouse or parent knowing in his or her heart that something is terribly wrong isn't a coincidence, because people can have a sixth sense when it comes to loved ones being in danger. A hero or heroine surviving a violent trauma isn't a contrivance. The will to live gives humans incredible strength to hang on to life. And the coincidences found in novels are not unrealistic in real life either. Being in the right place at the right time is the prologue of many real-life success stories.

The discerning hero or heroine is cautious of suspicious coincidences. They pay close attention to the words and actions of others. This applies in life, too. Have you ever heard a man explaining to his wife something like, "But I didn't know she'd be there," expecting his wife to believe that his ex's arrival was pure chance. Maybe the wife's intuitive reaction tells her otherwise. Children and teenagers also tell us tales of happenstance that we tend to doubt. Police officers hear such excuses all the time. For some reason, coincidences are not believable. They sound fake and insult our intelligence, leading us to be skeptical about the other things we've been told. These illogical circumstances are not the kind found in romances.

Romance novels are not about coincidences or contrivances, they're about instincts and learning to trust this inherent tool of survival. We all have this asset, but not everyone uses it. Readers of romance novels know its value. We recognize our women's intuition, too.

Like the wise hero and heroine, be wary of coincidences in your life. But when they're all you have to go by, believe in your hunches. Trust yourself to make good decisions.

I grew up reading romance books. They are like old friends to me. Then and now, romance books are a reaffirmation of the existence of love and the power of love. Romance books are a good read with something extra—perhaps a touch of magic.

—Joyce Adams

The cowboy lover can be irresistible

23

*Has anyone ever told you that you have a
very hard head beneath that cowboy hat?*

—JoAnn Ross, Hunk of the Month

Are cowboys an endangered species? What ever happened to those rugged men who weren't afraid to grab the bull by the horns? Have all those tough guys vanished? No. They are living and breathing in the heartland of America—and in romance novels. A close examination of cowboy stories shows that it's not just their sexy ruggedness that makes them so appealing.

There's more to a cowboy than meets the eye. Look at his surroundings. It's a rough, often harsh environment. The hours are demanding. It's a hands-on kind of job. The cowboy has to have stamina, be physically strong, mentally capable. He takes charge of land, livestock, and people. He doesn't put up with excuses. In other words, a cowboy is no wimp: He's a man's man, he's a decision maker, he knows what needs to be done.

Digging deeper beneath the layers of this man, we find what these traits imply. He's not afraid of the elements. He respects Mother Nature and can handle himself in the gravest situations. He's a survivor.

If he'll perform his work rain or shine, if he can persist with the grueling tasks day after day, if he can handle some unpleasantness and still keep making things work, then he's a man who can be counted on. He won't balk when things go wrong—he'll try to fix it. A cowboy won't run off at the first sign of trouble. He'll stick with you through thick and thin. If a woman hooks up with him, she'll survive, too. He'll protect her and the children.

JoAnn Ross defines a cowboy perfectly in *Hunk of the Month*. "Lucky's always been a rock. As solid as granite and every bit as hard to move. Family and the ranch have always been the two things he truly cares about."

In his daily routine he faces things head on—there's no time for beating around the bush—and he brings this frankness to a relationship. He isn't a man to discuss his feelings because he's too busy taking care of business to worry about emotions, so he might not be as sensitive or romantic as we'd like. Perhaps he doesn't know how to say the right things—but who wouldn't prefer a man who shows his affection over one who just says what he thinks a woman wants to hear?

Also, there's a sense of the wild in a cowboy, a man unbridled in his actions and responses. Just as he works hard, he loves hard, earnestly, intensely. There's promise of passionate lovemaking. Whoa, a cowboy isn't for every woman, but the right woman can spin the spurs of fate.

If there's one thing that can turn a cowboy for a loop, it's a woman. The only creature that won't jump at his orders. The one who'll stand up to him and tame him. But how can two people who don't see eye-to-eye be attracted to one another? She knows his tough side but she also glimpses his soft side when he gingerly treats an injured calf. There's two sides to him and both are necessary to make him the fine man he is. The heroine brings out the good in him. She settles him down by fulfilling his needs and letting him fulfill her needs.

She might have disagreements with him but he's a man who can be trusted. He doesn't lie, cheat, or steal. His handshake is as good as money in the bank. He'll learn how to treat her like a lady instead of a cowhand and she'll feel cherished in his strong arms. He'll remain devoted to that special woman and his family. She can't be afraid of hard work; she has to be strong mentally and physically, too. Ranches are no place for wimps of either sex.

To sum up, cowboys represent all that is good in America. He works hard, he's honest, he's passionate. While we all can't go out and rope a cowboy, I believe there's a bit of cowboy in every man. Yours might not wear a Stetson, but he's got that rugged, primal nature burning inside. It's your job to recognize that flame and love him for it, then tame him.

It makes me furious that the Romance genre is denigrated by so many people who have no idea what they're talking about, since many of our detractors admit to never having read one. Over the years I've received lots of letters from readers proving how valuable the genre is. One letter told me that one of my books was read over and over to a woman who was dying. The person who wrote said, 'Your book helped make her passing easier.' Another letter was from a widow who empathized with a character in one of my books. She told me she 'laughed deep inside for the first time in ten years' since her husband passed away. Both letters had me in tears. I've done whole speeches on the power of the genre, exemplified by heartfelt reader letters written to me and other romance writers. I'm humbled by the power of the genre in its ability to entertain, comfort and heal, and I'm proud to be a part of it.

—Renee Roszel

Keeping secrets leads to trouble 24

> He'd bared his soul to her, telling her his
> deepest, darkest secret, the thing he'd never
> told another person, and she hadn't turned
> away from him... Would the woman who'd held
> him in her arms and loved him so sweetly and
> so ardently after he'd exposed his shameful
> secret to her, turn away from him later
> because of that secret?
>
> **—Candace Schuler, The Mighty Quinn**

We all have secrets, some more explosive than others. However, our heroines and heroes hide humdingers. Their secrets put them through the wringer. Not only do they live with the consequences of their secrets on their own, but when their quandaries are discovered, they have a considerable price to pay.

In the case of a baby kept secret from the natural father, after the hero recovers from his initial shock, he blows up with anger. I've never read a book on this topic where the hero reacts mildly. His fury causes him to retaliate for being kept in the dark. He can't forgive her for lying to him, for keeping him from his own flesh and blood. Whatever his part in preventing her from telling him that he fathered a child, he lays the blame on her, proclaiming her actions unforgivable. He's filled with resentment at having lost out on precious moments of his child's life, watching him or her grow.

We momentarily feel sorry for him. We can see his point. Then we remember the heroine's reasons for hiding her baby and we feel the outrage she does. The audacity of the hero—he has no one to blame but himself. After all, he led the heroine to believe she was on her own.

With all this anger, blame, and opening of old wounds, how do these two hurt people get back together? The baby brings them together, the same baby that split them apart. That very innocent reminder of the love they once shared is the catalyst to make love bloom again. The heroine keeps a close eye on the hero when he's near her baby. Because father and child get along so well, she wonders if she made a mistake by not telling him about their baby. He's impressed by how well she is raising their child. He feels remorse that she did all right without him. Maybe she did what she thought she had to do.

Mother Nature helps the three bond. Parental instincts and bygone passions fuse. Their desire heightens as their trust builds. All they have to do is clear the emotional roadblocks from the past so they can travel any road they choose.

In Barbara Freethy's book *Daniel's Gift*, the heroine faces the ramifications of keeping her 'secret baby' in this moment of truth: "Jenny wanted to run and hide. Better yet, she wanted to wake up from this horrible nightmare that was becoming her reality... He was at her side, his hands strong on her waist as she started to crumple. What a coward I am, she thought as she was going down. Fainting like some spoiled, pampered woman instead of acting like the tough, single mother she was."

These wonderful secret baby stories take me through the wringer, too. Every emotion comes out: rage, betrayal, bitterness, shock, tenderness, respect, love. These books provide a roller coaster ride—up, down, forward, backward, they're exhausting to read. But that makes the ending all the more savory.

In the case of the secret pregnancy, the hero and heroine go through even more turmoil. The elements of denial, rejection, panic, and uncertainty are thrown into the gyrating mix. It's a wonder heroes and heroines don't have mental breakdowns.

Any secret kept is a secret that may one day blow up with more force than if it had been let into the open. Our heroines almost always carry a hefty weight on their shoulders, feel remorse, pay heavily in the future, and risk it all a second time. Our heroes almost always react with resentment, blame others, insert themselves into their child's lives, feel remorse, and learn the power of Mother Nature. And that's for stories with a happy ending!

When it's her only option, the heroine tends to carry the burden alone. While this makes for great fictional stories of extraordinary strength, in real life, keeping such major secrets can be overwhelming. I think most romance novel heroes and heroines would agree, keeping a significant secret isn't the best way to go. A better option is to follow the hero in Candace Schuler's *The Mighty Quinn,* who decides that, even though revealing his secret doesn't mean that his grief will go away, he'd rather be honest and do all he can to create a fresh start.

Personally speaking, I believe that I was drawn to romance because of its message of hope. People, whether unhappy or downtrodden or beat up by life, find hope in the romances we write. Naturally, the hope I speak of is Love. In our stories, our characters always and inevitably discover love, which, although it may not be the cure for a life of misery, it is, to my mind, a promise of a brighter future. Any of us can find love. Any of us can find that one special person who is meant for us. Romance offers us this hope. And for that, I am grateful.

—Casey Claybourne

We all want to forget something

*He had filled her thoughts for years, still
haunted her dreams at night, and he couldn't
even remember her! Had their association
been so meaningless to him that he couldn't
even place her face?... He had been her
husband, for heaven's sake, and now he only
asked if they'd met somewhere?*

—Barbara McMahon, One Love Forever

Did someone say amnesia? Who wouldn't like to forget all
their worries and get a fresh start? The amnesia victim gets to
do just that—walk away from her past. She isn't burdened
with guilt, regret, or loss. There's no concern about cleaning
out the garage, paying off credit cards, or returning to a stress-
ful job. On the down side though, sometimes the past was
wonderful and the present lonely. There's something missing
from her life and she doesn't know what it is. Her ghosts have
no faces but they haunt her nevertheless. Her misery comes
from not remembering.

All the same, it's intriguing to speculate about amnesia happening to us. Would our husbands go beyond the call of duty

to find us? If so, would we fall in love all over again? Wouldn't that be romantic—to know that you were really meant for each other? He'd have to sweep you off your feet again, court you, chase you. Hey, it might be worth the bump on the head to find out. And if it doesn't work, you won't remember him anyway because you'll have amnesia.

The most 'memorable' amnesia novels are the ones where the couples fall head over heels in love—for the first time—again. One mate turns up out of the blue to rescue the amnesiac. Or the amnesiac returns to the place that's in his heart, rocking the world of the one he walked out on. The one with amnesia goes through a convoluted emotional ride. Something draws them to the stranger, something instinctual. The feeling creates a wariness and an excitement. To further complicate things, the stranger knows things about them, deep secrets.

Imagine if it happened to you. The man is attractive, he's a stranger, you feel connected to him, and you have a spontaneous desire for him. Then he shocks the heck out of you by knowing some of your deepest yearnings. Would your impulse make you run or stay and learn more about him? Our heroes and heroines don't have a choice—their partner pursues them until fate turns on their side. It's their destiny to fall in love again.

But reuniting isn't without difficulty. In Jodi O'Donnell's *A Man To Remember*, the heroine is engaged to another man when the hero finally finds her. In Elizabeth August's *The Forgotten Husband*, the heroine is led to believe her marriage to the hero was a mistake. These couples have to start from square one to rebuild their relationships.

Maybe that's the appeal of amnesia stories—they show us how to start over with the man in our lives. They demonstrate how to progress beyond troubled pasts or unspoken resentment. We learn, undoubtedly, that love has the power to defeat all difficulties, even those buried deep in our minds.

Reading a romance novel, especially a well-written historical adventure, gives me a measure of relaxation that none other pastime can. I can lose myself for days in a thick, entertaining book that transports me to another era and captivates me with a love story that keeps me turning the pages. Some say these are just fairy tales for women, but there are many times in life when people need some form of escape. Listening to the news every night is enough to get anyone uptight. What form of relaxation people choose is up to the individual. As for me, I'll take historical romance any day.

—**Kathleen E. Woodiwiss**

100% genuine commitment is the goal

26

> There were pieces of him up there floating among
> the stars, but most of him was inside her still,
> where he belonged. For she had stolen his soul,
> this woman, his wife. He would never fully belong
> to himself again. "Cariad," he whispered in Welsh,
> a word he didn't know he knew, a word he couldn't
> remember hearing. But he knew what it meant...
> beloved.

—Penelope Williamson, Keeper of the Dream

Sure, romance novels can have Cinderella plots where a prince, tycoon, or celebrity sweeps a woman off her feet. In romances there can be magical elements, ghosts or angels. Naturally countless romances are ground in reality, but even those that intertwine fantasy within them have this aspect in common: It's not the noble title, the pot of gold, nor the castle filled with servants that lures the heroine. It's not having magical powers or winged friends. The real fantasy is a relationship with 100 percent commitment.

Before a romance novel ends, the hero and heroine make a commitment to each other. Their love is so powerful, their bond so strong, that we have no doubts that this relationship will last no matter what.

This is the goal for readers, too. Who wouldn't want that kind of promise for an enduring, exuberant love forever? Just as our heroines lead hectic, unpredictable lives, so do we. It's reassuring to read about love that lasts, people who make it work, people who find time for romance. An affectionate, supportive, steadfast relationship is a dream come true.

Unquestionably many readers are already in a relationship with the man they love with all their heart. But that old stinker, time, and the lack thereof, doesn't allow for bonding, romancing, and other things we'd like to do together. That doesn't mean we don't cherish our lifelong partner or view him any less. Treasure those moments you do have. Make time to create new memories.

Reading romances reminds me of the times when my husband courted me, the thrill of falling in love, and the strong love we have for each other. Reading them keeps the kindle glowing in me. These books prompt me to recognize that working things out is better than separating. Like ours, their relationships aren't perfect, but they work to keep the intimacy thriving. I figure, if the characters' love can survive, ours can too. Romance novels also bring to mind the errors we can make and the chaos we can get ourselves into—and, of course, how being courageous can get us out of such predicaments.

While we may identify with and admire the tenacity of the hero and heroine in romance novels, we really want to read about a man and woman finding a love that will last a lifetime. No matter how many stories we read, this is the ending we anticipate. We read romances one after the other, yet each ending touches us in a different way because the characters, their situation, and that spark of magic the story inspires are all unique. It triggers something deep-seated, a natural yearning perhaps, for that kind of bond with another human being that is very assuring and seductive. Can we have that in our lives?

If you want to deepen the bond with your mate, it takes commitment. If you want his emotional, physical, and spiritual devotion, you have to devote yourself to him. If you want her complete loyalty, you must be totally loyal to her. This isn't necessarily easy to do, but you must be willing to give what you want to receive.

Romances imply that you have the power within you to take control of your future. If you want a relationship with 100 percent commitment, it's up to you. The love you want doesn't have to be a fantasy.

I often refer to romance novels as those special books that heal. Not only do these books offer hope but they often touch the reader on deep, personal levels of emotion. The stories bring two strong and honorable people together, one man and one woman. How they solve the conflicts that endanger their relationship, learn to overcome fear and grow into better people, is the story's main focus. As the last page turns, the reader knows that this kind of love will endure until the end of time. And that's why at the end of a wonderfully satisfying love story there's an "aaaaaaahhhhhhhhhh..."

—Linda Hill

$\mathscr{L}$ove changes everything

27

> *"If you marry for love and not money," Paco was*
> *saying, "you'll have good nights and bad days."*
> *"In my opinion," one of the others said, "love is a*
> *ghost. Everyone talks about it, but few have seen it."*

—Carol Grace, Home Is Where the Heart Is

A confirmed bachelor can have his world turned upside down by love. Everyone says, "she really changed him," but he's still the same man. Only his priorities have changed. He has gone from thinking mainly about himself or his work to considering another person. The same holds true for a confirmed bachelorette—she evolves from satisfying her own wants and desires to worrying about her beloved. Suddenly they can't envision a future without the other.

Love affects a person from the inside out. There's a new sense of purpose in his thinking, a crazy grin on his lips, a sparkle in his eyes. We only have to look at him to know he's in love.

Love truly does make the sunshine warmer, flowers bloom brighter, the air smell fresher, and food taste better. Even our bodies look better—we feel beautiful. Being in love makes the world seem less threatening, and brings pleasure to the simplest of things. The joy of sharing things with our loved ones—our hobbies, duties, opinions, and intimacy—are limitless. (Not our chocolate though, some things aren't meant to be shared!)

In romance novels, the characters are changed by the romance. It was unexpected; it's a complication for them. In a suspense, the stakes become higher if the person in danger is someone you love. In a time travel, the desire to get back home conflicts with the desire to stay with the lover. In a historical, the quest to forge ahead in an untamed frontier battles with the desire to keep loved ones safe. Through the course of the story, everything changes.

For the wary hero in Carol Grace's novel *Mail-Order Male*, falling in love interferes with his conceived preference for solitude: "'There he is,' she said at last, 'in the fir tree. I wonder what he's looking for.' 'It sounds like a mating call to me,' he muttered. He ought to know. If he were an owl he'd be out there calling, too. It was a sure sign of spring, the male of the species looking for the female. Max had found the female he was looking for; she was right here in this room."

Many heroes and heroines have been led kicking and screaming down the road of love. They resisted romance and the responsibilities that come with it. But once hooked, it's all over but the ceremony. Once love strikes, their priorities will never be the same.

The hero in Sierra Rydell's *On Middle Ground*, set in the remote Alaskan wilderness, endured great internal turmoil to reach this point: "Soon they would be married. Soon they would build a new home, a larger place for a growing family. This spring would indeed be a time of renewal and rebirth. And though he would continue to walk the middle ground, now he had a companion, a woman whose needs met his and whose needs he wanted to meet. Together they would face the challenges of the future, melding the traditional with the modern, the past with the present."

In reality as in romantic fiction, love gives us the will to persist, the strength to survive, the courage to face the truth. Love lets us smile at the small annoyances, and things that once bothered us no longer seem important. Love allows us to appreciate the ordinary. As romance novels demonstrate to us, we really don't need extravagances, daredevil pastimes, or ritzy parties to keep us happy. Just a cozy home, a warm hug, and lots of love—these things can make us feel extraordinary.

When I was a reporter, I always wanted to change the facts of a story so it could have a happy ending. That is what drives me to write romance fiction now—that consuming need to have all loose ends tied up, and to see couples walk off into the sunset together, eternally youthful, healthy, and ecstatically in love.

—Karen Leabo

Romance revives the spirit

Taking a virgin mistress was proving to be every bit as arduous and involved a process as taking a virgin bride. That annoying conclusion occurred to Pierce on the third day of his bizarre courtship as he stalked up and down Regent Street, going from shop to shop, searching for a gift suitable for his mistress-to-be...this romance business was nothing short of exhausting.

—Betina Krahn, The Perfect Mistress

As we watch heroes and heroines strive for true love, we see them step outside of their boundaries and blossom before our eyes. Romance does that to them. Romance ignites the heart and rejuvenates the spirit. It's what makes people walk with a bounce, smile from within, and feel hope for the future.

A movie I admire, *Dead Poets Society*, has a scene that really touches me. The English teacher huddles his college prep students together and tells them that law, engineering, and medicine are all fine professions, but love, romance, is what we live for. I feel that sums up the power of romance novels. People want a career, a house of their own, travel, and adventure—all the things associated with the American Dream. But the one achievement that makes life so delicious is love.

Love gives us a boost to tackle demanding careers. Romance is what makes travel and adventure exciting. And the prevalent American Dream includes a house, a spouse, two children, and a dog. Whether we know it or not, love and romance are ingrained into our dreams and expectations. Like an array of computer codes, we're programmed to pair with one another. In today's society that means marriage. What's marriage without romance? In my opinion, it's Peg and Al Bundy (of television's *Married, With Children*). Yes, these two love each other, but his idea of romance is beer and a bowling alley. Her idea of romance is spending his money.

That's not exactly what most women want. Admit it, we want the bubbly champagne and red roses. We're thrilled with love notes written by our spouses. We'd like to believe our legs will still weaken and our blood boil from a passionate kiss even after 30 years of marriage. We all hope we'll remain seductresses to our Casanovas long after we have grandchildren. Flirting with our spouses is not only romantic, it's fun.

But romance is other things, too. A sincere compliment warms our hearts, a smile tingles our toes, a certain look takes our breath away. Romance is having eyes only for each other.

Romance novels stir these sentiments and impel us to let our imaginations loose and speculate about dilemmas we don't want in our lives but that are fascinating to read about. In Johanna Lindsey's novel *Say You Love Me*, the heroine is sold at auction to pay the family's debts. What real-life woman would want to face such an ordeal? No one I know. Yet we are drawn into the story by a heroine we care about. Can she overcome this indignity? We are relieved to find that the man who purchases her is heroic, then we care about him, too.

Ah, romance novels. They bring us assurance that men will be men and women will be women, regardless of how much civilization changes. Romance novels bring us to laughter or despair, they enlighten us, they bring us scintillating sex and quiet moments of introspection. Romance novels show us how to keep love alive, our spirits young, and our hearts light because romance, as a frequent practice, reinforces love. Romantic gestures are an expression of love. With love on our side we can soar. At least that's how our mates make us feel—like we can do anything. Someone who loves you is someone who believes in you, and that belief gives you profound powers.

That's a reason we want the romance to continue. We don't just want to fall in love, we want to be in love for the rest of our lives. And romance keeps the fires burning. As the hero in Betina Krahn's *The Perfect Mistress* discovers, romance can be exhausting, but the results are worth it. Romance is balm for the spirit.

Romance novels are therapy for the soul. They suggest to each of us that working to keep love new and exciting does indeed revive the spirit.

Writing romance allows me to express my own belief in faith, hope, and the enduring power of love to bring about a happy ending.

—Teresa Medeiros

Happy endings are for real 29

You are the only woman I have ever asked
to marry me. You are everything I want and
need in a wife, and I knew it the minute I
saw you. We are in this together, you and I.
We will make it work. You have my word of
honor on it.

—Jayne Ann Krentz, The Wedding Night

Everyday people like you and me can live happily ever after, too. We all deserve it, no matter our backgrounds or pasts. Whether we're single, married, divorced, or widowed, we can lead zesty, fulfilling lives. We can have it all, because happy endings are created by the persons involved.

But having it all may result in being too worn out to be romantic. Once you achieve your dreams, remember the most important part of maintaining success is enjoying what you worked so hard for. Nourish all the areas of your life. Take care of your body and spirit, then you'll have the energy to be a feisty heroine of boundless vitality, ideas, wit, and poise. Oh, and you can be sexy, too.

Also, remember that happiness in a relationship doesn't rest soley on your shoulders. Don't let your mate slack off. It takes two to tango and two to make a happily ever after. When both people are committed to making things work, beautiful things will happen in the relationship.

Truthfully, things aren't always sunshine and laughter. Like in romance novels, we all have our setbacks and disappointments. The secret is to press beyond the tough times. While life may not truly be like romance novels, we can learn from them by seeing characters work through their problems. Romance novels can teach us how to replace a sad ending with a happy one.

While for many of us hearing the man of our dreams profess his love and devotion is the passage to a happy ending, for others, a happy ending doesn't include matrimony. A satisfying outcome could be self-acceptance or the attainment of a long-awaited goal. That's perfectly acceptable, too. Being happy is a matter of not relying on others to bring you happiness.

Be content with yourself. It'll be contagious, as are the underlying messages between the lines of the stories we love to read. The messages are: Take responsibility for your actions, be strong, have a good heart, and be yourself. The theme in romance novels always includes women having inner strength.

When we read about strong women over and over, novel after novel, this concept is bound to affect us. No wonder these books are so powerful; they touch us personally. They color our way of looking at ourselves and the world.

Romance novels are here to stay. They deliver more than stories of love. They include knowledge of the human spirit. We can all learn from the wisdom within the pages of romance novels.

Like heroes and heroines, do your best with what you have; listen to your heart and trust your instincts. Find time for romance. It's the start of a future that begins with...happily ever after.

Appendix I

Types of Romance Novels

If you're already a romance novel enthusiast, you probably have your favorite subgenres and lines. I hope these descriptions inspire you to try others you might not have considered.

Traditional: Also referred to as sweet romances, these books have little or no profanity and couples do not have sex unless they are married. Even then, lovemaking scenes are not described in the same detail found in other romances. Still, these books can be high in sexual tension. They are uplifting contemporary stories that cover a wide range, from serious to humorous and fantasy to reality. Publishers/lines include Harlequin Romance and Silhouette Romance. A traditional publisher for libraries is Avalon Books.

Young Adult: These novels have teenage characters and deal with adolescent love. As you know, adolescence is a time of great emotional upheaval and these books reflect that. They are reality based and can include real issues or just the magic of falling in love for the first time. Publishers include Avon, Bantam, Bethany House, Parachute Press, and Scholastic.

Series Contemporary: These are the sexy books. The love scenes are often presented in a sensual manner, making them all the more scintillating. The longer books may comprise very involved plots and secondary characters. They contain an extensive selection of tone, pacing, reality, suspense, and humor. Publishers/lines include Bantam Loveswept; Harlequin Presents, Temptation, American, and Superromance; Silhouette Desire, Special Edition, and Intimate Moments; and Kensington Precious Gem.

Single Title Contemporary: These romance novels are the big books. Some may be released in hardcover first. Anything goes with these more involved stories. They can be gritty, intense, humorous, heartwarming, or sexy, or may contain paranormal elements.

However, the romance is the intricate fiber woven throughout the novel. Publishers include Avon, Arabesque, Ballantine/Fawcett, Bantam, Berkley/Jove, Dell, Harper, Mira, Pocket, Scarlet, St. Martin's Press, Indigo, and Warner.

Historical: Besides taking place in the past, these books are frequently quite provocative. While historical facts are accurate, readers get a true sense of time and place through sensory details, as experienced by the characters, not history book descriptions. Publishers/lines include Avon, Bantam, Berkley/Jove, Dell, Harlequin, Leisure, Love Spell, Pocket, St. Martin's Press, Topaz, Warner, and Zebra.

Regency: These novels can be sweet like the traditionals or hot and spicy. They are set in Europe during the Regency era, primarily the early 1800s. They are rich in period flavor and mindset. Publishers include Fawcett, Harlequin, Signet, St. Martin's Press, and Zebra.

Inspirational: There is no profanity or graphic sexuality. These novels blend Christian values, faith, and spirituality with the romance story. Publishers include Barbour, Bethany House, Multnomah, Steeple Hill, Tyndale, and Waterbrook Press.

Multicultural: These books are romances portraying characters of color. They include the nuances of background, traditions and expressions of the characters' culture. Publishers/lines include Indigo and Kensington's Arabesque and Encanto lines.

Suspense: Previously known as Gothics, the romantic suspense novel includes elements of mystery, danger, foul play, and impending doom. These novels are reality based and some stories can be violent, others light. The romance increases the tension. Although any of the single title or series publishers may publish suspense, the only one with a specific suspense line is Harlequin Intrigue. Avalon Books also consistently publishes two romantic mysteries every other month.

Paranormal: Romantic stories that include elements of the supernatural, such as ghosts, angels, vampires, werewolves, witchcraft, wizardry, reincarnation, or time travel. They can be set in the past, present, or future. As with all of the above categories, the romance is integral to the story. Any of the previously mentioned publishers of single title or historical releases may publish a paranormal book. Those with specific paranormal lines include Berkley's Haunting Hearts and Jove's Time Passages lines, and Leisure's Love Spell/Time Swept line.

Anthologies: An anthology is a collection of novellas, shorter stories of between 25,000 and 30,000 words each. Each collection is usually based on a specific theme or place. Generally, several romance authors contribute one story. Sensuality level varies with each publisher.

Appendix II

Romance Novels Published

Overall, the number of romance novels released has risen over the last four years, most likely a response to increasing interest in the genre.

PUBLISHER	1994	1995	1996	1997
Avon	80	68	83	138
Avalon	36	36	36	36
Ballantine	6	5	6	6
Bantam	106	84	99	156
Barbour	48	48	52	55
Berkley/Jove	90	63	67	126
Bethany House	24	24	24	25
Delacorte	3	2	2	6
Dell	29	25	28	72
Fawcett	38	30	39	60
Harper	88	79	63	30
Harlequin	424	493	471	570
Genesis/Indigo	0	4	8	12
Kensington	4	8	12	12
Leisure	142	133	99	100
Mira	12	48	45	48
Multnomah	0	6	16	16
NAL/Signet	87	91	106	142
Pinnacle/Arabesque	54	68	68	86
Pocket	40	44	55	60
Silhouette	348	325	351	552
St. Martin's Press	13	19	34	66
Tyndale	2	16	16	12
Warner	10	22	20	30
Zebra	202	176	207	242
TOTAL	1,886	1,917	2,007	2,658

Data reported in The Romance Writer's Report, a publication of the Romance Writer's of America. Issues used: Vol. 15, No. 6, Nov-Dec, 1995; Vol. 16, No. 3, April 1996; Vol. 17, No. 6, June 1997; Vol. 18, No. 6, June 1998

Appendix III

Romance Publishers' Web Sites

Most romance publishers have wonderful sites for displaying their books and authors. Visiting these sites is a great way to keep up on your favorite authors' newest releases.

AVALON BOOKS: http://www.avalonbooks.com

A fun, whimsical site. Nice author interviews.

AVON: http://www.avonbooks.com/avon/romance.html

Great site includes a Datebook in Romantic History, new and upcoming novel excerpts, and the opportunity to vote for hero of the month.

BALLANTINE/FAWCETT: http://www.randomhouse.com/BB/loveletters

Includes Indigo imprint. This fine site has nice excerpts, lists more books by author, and includes reader reviews and read-a-chapter.

BANTAM DOUBLEDAY DELL: http://www.bdd.com/romance

Great site has a 'search by author' feature, offers the ability to e-mail favorite author, and lists author tours, new novel excerpts, and reviews.

BERKLEY/JOVE: http://www.penguinputnam.com/catalog/index.html
(Choose category: Fiction; Select: Romance)

Includes Signet Regencies and Topaz. Provides preview of books.

DORCHESTER: http://www.dorchesterpub.com

Includes Leisure Books and Love Spell. Very nice site, with meet the author area, and great book descriptions.

HARLEQUIN/SILHOUETTE: http://www.romance.net

Very nice site. Annual romance survey, horoscope, discussion forums, new books description, and featured author section.

HARDSHELL WORD FACTORY: http://www.Hardshell.com/romance.html

Electronic publisher. Gives description of books, with nice excerpts and reviews.

HARPER: http://www.harpercollins.com/books/index.html (Select: Romance)

Gives descriptions of their books.

LIONHEARTED: http://www.lionhearted.com

Previews and book reviews.

NEW CONCEPTS PUBLISHING: http://www.newconceptspublishing.com

Electronic publisher. Has author biography section, excerpts, and reviews.

POCKET: http://www.simonsays.com/catalog/options.cgi (Select: Romance)

Limited links to authors' web sites, book excerpt, and other titles by author.

ST. MARTIN'S PRESS: http://www.stmartins.com (Select: St Martin's Paperbacks)

Gives preview of book, reviews, and author tour information.

ZEBRA: http://www.zebrabooks.com/

Kensington Publishing's site, which also includes Arabesque, Encanto, and Pinnacle. Best site—with author contact page, you can send fan mail and read author biography. Offers author appearance schedule, author interviews, links to web sites, schedule of 'chat with' sessions, nice preview of books.

Appendix IV

Interesting Romance-Related Web Sites

There are many web sites for romance buffs. I selected ones that concentrate on romance novels. Most of these sites have links to other entertaining sites.

http://www.theromancereader.com

Features reviews and news about romance authors. Freebies from authors.

http://www.romanceweb.com

Author links and book reviews.

http://www.icgnet.com/romancebooks/

The Ultimate Internet Romance Book Site. Great listing of books by theme, with a gallery of book covers, cover models, and book collecting tips and facts.

http://www.affairedecoeur.com/index.html

Affaire de Coeur magazine includes book reviews and a 'Nan Knows' column.

http://www.likesbooks.com/

All About Romance site. Nice Castle of the Week column. Fun articles from readers. Excellent element to site is 'If you like... Then try...' function, which recommends similar style of authors.

http://www.romantictimes.com

Romantic Times magazine page. Reviews and top picks for recommended reading. Includes reader reviews and author awards list. (Magazine articles and author profiles require subscription fee.)

http://www.geocities.com/Paris/LeftBank/6143

The Chivalric Gentleman Page. Includes great quotes on love, romantic ideas, a variety of links, and much more.

http://www.msms.doc.k12.ms.us/~ebaldwin/jane.html

Nice site for Jane Austen fans, which includes Jane Austen novel quotes, favorite scenes, and an index of Austen characters.

http://www.plaza.interport.net/romanceforever/index.html

Romance Forever online magazine site. Includes a Special Moment of Romance feature, a Hear Ye, Hear Ye column, featuring news about authors, along with reviews and interviews.

http://weber.u.washington.edu/~ramirez/romance.htm

Romance 101 site, including inspiration, humor, Random Acts of Romance, and Lessons in Love.

http://www.poboxes.com/MaxSales

Sneak Previews of Romance & Women's Fiction, with featured authors and links to web sites of current and previously featured authors.

http://www.geocities.com/~bookbug/home.html

Listing of novels by theme—romantic comedy, ghost, or angel—and gives excerpts. Includes reader polls, book buzz reviews, and author home pages.

http://www.thekiss.com

Fun site with tips on kissing and much more.

http://www.booktalk.com

Includes fantastic features on romance authors, intriguing articles by authors of all genres, book buzz, and more.

http://www.literary-liaisons.com

For historical romance fans, this site features "On this day in history," a great listing of RWA Chapters Online, and wonderful research articles.

http://www.romanceforum.com

The Romance Readers and Writers Forum site, with industry news, author interviews, author's pages, and contests. Also traces hard-to-find-books.

Appendix V

Romance Authors' Web Sites, Addresses, and Publishers

Shana Abé
http://www.tlt.com/authors/sabe.htm
e-mail: ShanaAbe@aol.com
Bantam Books–Historical

Trisha Alexander
e-mail: trisha@pdq.net
Silhouette Special Edition

Victoria Alexander
http://www.eclectics.com/victoria
e-mail: VictAlex@aol.com
P.O. Box 31544, Omaha, NE 68131
Leisure (Love Spell and Historical)

Heather Allison
(aka Heather MacAllister)
http://www.flash.net/~hmac
e-mail: hmac@flash.net
Harlequin (Romance and Temptation)

Rosalyn Alsobrook
http://home.earthlink.net/~ralsobrook/
P.O. Box 195, Gilmer, TX 75644
Harlequin American, Pinnacle, St. Martin's
Press, Tower, and Zebra

Gloria Alvarez
P.O. Box 740274, New Orleans, LA 70174
Kensington (Precious Gem and Encanto)

Susan Amarillas
http://www.apayne.com/susanamarillas
Harlequin Historical

Laurel Ames (aka Barb Miller)
e-mail: scribe@cvzoom.net
RD 6 Box 774, Mt. Pleasant, PA 15666
Harlequin (Historical and Regency)

Shari Anton
http://www.eclectics.com/sharianton
e-mail: j-s-antoni@worldnet.att.net
P.O. Box 510611
New Berlin, WI 53151-0611
Harlequin Historical

Lisa E. Arlt
http://www.pobox.com/~LisaArlt
e-mail: LisaArlt@Pobox.Com
Harlequin Temptation

Anne Avery
e-mail: anneavery@pcisys.net
P.O. Box 62533
Colorado Springs, CO 80962-2533
Leisure, Topaz, and Bantam

Laura Baker
e-mail: lbaker10@aol.com
P.O. Box 23203
Albuquerque, NM 87192
St. Martin's Press

Madeline Baker (aka Amanda Ashley)
http://www.whittierca.com/mbaker.htm
e-mail: DarkWritr@aol.com
P.O. Box 1703, Whittier, CA 90609-1703
Leisure, Love Spell, and Topaz

Becky Barker
http://members.aol.com/bekybarker/index.html
P.O. Box 113, Mt. Sterling, OH 43143
Dell, Meteor, Silhouette Intimate Moments,
and Kensington Precious Gem

Jill Barnett
http://www.romanceweb.com/jillbarnett
P.O. Box 8166, Fremont, CA 94537
Pocket Books

**Victoria Barrett (aka Victoria Cole and
Vicki Hinze)**
http://www.vickihinze.com
St. Martin's Press, Pinnacle, and Silhouette

Stephanie Bartlett
e-mail: stbartle@orednet.org
Kensington and Bantam

Pamela Bauer
c/o Midwest Fiction Writers
P.O. Box 47888, Plymouth, MN 55447
Harlequin (American, Superromance,
and Romance); as Pamela Jerrold:
Silhouette Special Edition

Donna Bell
e-mail: dendon@gte.net
Pageant Books, Jove, and Zebra Books

Jo Beverley
http://www.sff.net/people/jobeverley
e-mail: jobeverley@poboxes.com
c/o The Alice Orr Agency,
305 Madison Ave., Suite 1166
New York, NY 10165
Avon (Regency and Historical), Penguin–Topaz,
Walker, and Zebra (Regency and Historical)

Jane Bierce
http://hickory.engr.utk.edu/~ellis/jane.html
e-mail: janecb@vic.com
Harlequin American,
Silhouette Romance, Zebra,
and Hard Shell Word Factory

**Cheryl Biggs (aka Cherlyn Biggs
and Cherlyn Jac)**
e-mail: JBiggs@att.net
Silhouette Intimate Moments, Kensington
Historical, and Zebra; as Cherlyn Biggs:
Bantam Loveswept; as Cherlyn Jac: Harper

Sonya Birmingham
http://www.flash.net/~sonyab
e-mail: sonyab@flash.net
Avon Historical and Leisure Books

Rosanne Bittner
http://www.parrett.net/~bittner
e-mail: bittner@parrett.net
P.O. Box 1044, Coloma, Michigan 49038
Zebra Books, Bantam Books, Forge Books,
St. Martin's Press, and Jove Books

Jennifer Blake
http://www.jenniferblake.com
P.O. Box 9218, Quitman, LA 71268
Fawcett Books and Mira Books

Jane Bonander
http://www.booktalk.com/JBonander
e-mail: JBonander@aol.com
P.O. Box 10702, St. Paul, MN 55110
Avon Books, Pocket Books, Kensington
Precious Gem, and St. Martin's Press

Stephanie Bond
P.O. Box 2395, Alpharetta, GA 30023
Harlequin (Temptation and Love &
Laughter); as Stephanie Bancroft:
Bantam Loveswept

Elizabeth Boyle
http://www.wolfenet.com/~elizbo
P.O. Box 47252, Seattle, WA 98146
Dell

Laura Bradley
e-mail: Luvnmystry@aol.com
P.O. Box 780372,
San Antonio, TX 78278-0372
Robinson Scarlet

Jean Brashear
http://www.onr.com/user/bejean/brashear.html
P.O. Box 40012, Georgetown, TX 78628
Silhouette Special Edition

Terri Brisbin
e-mail: Tbrisbin@aol.com
P.O. Box 41, Berlin, NJ 08009-0041
Jove Time Passages

Suzanne Brockmann (aka Anne Brock)
e-mail: SFTHQ@aol.com
P.O. Box 5092, Wayland, MA 01778
Silhouette Intimate Moments, Ballantine,
Bantam Loveswept, Harlequin Intrigue,
Precious Gem; as Anne Brock: Pinnacle
and Meteor

Dixie Browning
e-mail: dixiebb@juno.com
Silhouette (Desire and Romance)

Margaret Brownley
http://www.sff.net:80/people/Margaret.Brownley
Topaz, Harlequin, and St. Martin's Press

Pamela Burford
http://www.home.eznet.net/~
patryan/pam/pburford.htm
e-mail: pambl@aol.com
P.O. Box 1321
North Baldwin, NY 11510-0721
Harlequin (Temptation and Intrigue)

Nancy Butler
e-mail: Fetchcat@aol.com
Signet Regencies

June Calvin
e-mail: jlwc@telepath.com
P.O. Box 60433
Oklahoma City, OK 73146-0433
Signet Regency

Stella Cameron
http://www.terran.org/pages/stella.cameron
e-mail: pushpen@aol.com
Kensington, Warner, and Zebra

K. N. Casper
http://www.geocities.com/Paris/
Rue/8040/casper.html
e-mail: littleoaks@juno.com
P.O. Box 4062, San Angelo, TX 76904
Harlequin Superromance

Christine Charles
e-mail: charlieg@sprintmail.com
P.O. Box 1764, Lee's Summit, MO 64063
Hard Shell Word Factory

Margaret (Meg) Chittenden
http://www.techline.com/~megc
e-mail: megc@techline.com OR
MegC3@aol.com
Ace Books, Harlequin (Superromance,
Temptation, and Dreamscape),
Pinnacle, and Worldwide

**Daphne Clair (aka Laurey Bright and
Clarissa Garland)**
http://www.voyager.co.nz/~dclair
P.O. Box 18240, Glen Innes
Auckland, New Zealand
Harlequin Mills & Boon; as Laurey Bright:
Silhouette; as Clarissa Garland:
Robinson Scarlet

Casey Claybourne
e-mail: CMickle@pacbell.net
P.O. Box 601706, Sacramento, CA 95860
Berkley/Jove and Jove Regency

Donna Clayton
http://www.tlt.com/authors/drw/htm
e-mail: DonnaFaz@aol.com
Silhouette Romance

Pat Cody
http://www.PatCody.com
e-mail: patcody@SWBell.net
P.O. Box 185451, Fort Worth, TX 76181
Harper Monogram and Leisure Historical

Colleen Collins
http://www.ecentral.com/members/
crw/CCOLLINS.HTM
Harlequin Love & Laughter

Lyn Cote
At Faith, Hope & Love Site:
http://www.webpak.net/~
robinlee/FHL/info.html
Steeple Hill Love Inspired

Ramona Crawford (aka Louise Crawford)
e-mail: wtgfeaver@aol.com
Kensington Precious Gem; as Louise
Crawford: New Concepts Publishing

Millie Criswell
http://www.1q.com/romance/millie
e-mail: MillieCris@AOL.com
P. O. Box 41206
Fredericksburg, VA 22404
Harper Collins, Pinnacle,
Warner Books, and Zebra Books

Jennifer Crusie
http://www.sff.net/people/jennifercrusie
Bantam Loveswept, Harlequin (Love & Laughter
and Temptation), and St. Martin's Press

Ruth Jean Dale
http://www.sff.net:80/people/Ruth.Jean.Dale
Harlequin and St. Martin's Press

Carole Dean
e-mail: esheedy@island.net
Kensington Publishing and Meteor

Shawna Delacorte
e-mail: prsp27a@prodigy.com OR
SharonDennison@prodigy.net
6505 E. Central, Box #300
Wichita, Kansas 67206-1924
Silhouette Desire, Yours Truly, and
Harlequin Intrigue

Janelle Denison
http://www.weluvromance.com
e-mail: janeldenison@earthlink.net
Harlequin (Temptation and Romance)

Jamie Denton
http://members.aol.com/
occauthor/jamiedenton
e-mail: dentonja@ndak.net
Harlequin (Superromance and Temptation)

Jean DeWitt
P.O. Box 15507
Beverly Hills, CA 90209-5507
HarperPaperbacks

Jennifer Dunne
http://members.aol.com/yeep
e-mail: Yeep@aol.com
P.O. Box 496, Endicott, NY 13761-0496
The FictionWorks (audio) and
New Concepts Publishing

Lois Faye Dyer
c/o Paperbacks Plus, 1618 Bay Street
Port Orchard, Washington 98366
Silhouette Special Edition, Kensington
Precious Gem, and Kismet

Kathleen Eagle
Home Page at Bookbug On The Web:
http://www.geocities.com/Athens/
Forum/8078/eagle.html
At The Avon Ladies:
http://www.judithivory.com/avonladies/
e-mail: KatEagle@aol.com
c/o Midwest Fiction Writers
P.O. Box 47888, Plymouth, MN 55447
Avon, Harlequin Historical, and Silhouette
(Special Edition and Intimate Moments)

Anne Eames
http://www.booksbyeames.com
e-mail: anne@booksbyeames.com
4217 Highland Rd. #252
Waterford, MI 48328
Silhouette Desire

Gail Eastwood
http://www.eclectics.com/gaileastwood/
P.O. Box 5252, Wakefield, RI 02880-0894
Signet Regency

Susan Edwards
http://members.aol.com/susanedw2u
e-mail: sedwards2u@aol.com
P.O. Box 766, Los Altos, CA 94023-0766
Leisure Historical

Jean Ross Ewing
http://www.rmi.net/~jrewing
e-mail: jrewing@rmi.net
Zebra Regency and Berkley Historical

Elisabeth Fairchild
http://biz.nstar.net/RGP/D-home.html
Signet Regency

Colleen Faulkner
517 Bridgeville Road
Seaford, Delaware 19973
Kensington Historical

Jo Ann Ferguson
(aka Joanna Hampton)
http://www.romcom.com/ferguson
e-mail: jaferg@erols.com
c/o RWA/NEC, P.O. Box 1667
Framingham, MA 01701-9998
Zebra Regency; as Joanna Hampton:
Berkley/Jove

Amy J. Fetzer
http://www.apayne.com/amyfetzer
e-mail: fetzer@hargray.com
P.O. Box 9241, Beaufort, SC 29904-9241
Silhouette Desire and Zebra

Liz Fielding
http://www.lizfield.demon.co.uk
e-mail: liz@lizfield.demon.co.uk
Harlequin (Romance and Mills & Boon) and
Robinson Scarlet

Connie Flynn (aka Casey Roberts)
http://home.att.net/~cflynn
e-mail: CFlynn@worldnet.att.net
7620 E. McKellips Rd., Suite 4202,
Scottsdale, AZ 85257
Harlequin Superromance, Silhouette Yours
Truly, Penguin Topaz, and Onyx

Suzanne Forster
http://www.blush.com
e-mail: sueforster@aol.com
P.O. Box 1034, Newport Beach, CA 92663
Bantam (Fanfare and Loveswept), Berkley,
Harlequin (Mira and Anthology) and
Silhouette (Desire and Romance)

Lori Foster
http://www.eclectics.com/lorifoster
e-mail: lorifoster@poboxes.com
Harlequin Temptation,
Silhouette Desire, and Berkley

Karen Fox
http://home.att.net/~foxje/
e-mail: foxje@worldnet.att.net
P.O. Box 31541
Colorado Springs, CO 80931-1541
Leisure Love Spell

Roz Denny Fox
e-mail: rdfox@worldnet.att.net
P.O. Box 17480-101, Tucson, AZ 85731
Harlequin

Barbara Freethy (aka Kristina Logan)
e-mail: Bafreethy@aol.com
P.O. Box 304, Burlingame, CA 94011-0304
Avon Books; as Kristina Logan: Silhouette
Romance

Kate Freiman
http://www.romanceweb.com/kfreiman
At Canadian Romance Authors Network:
http://www.vgrant.com/cran.htm
e-mail: kate_freiman@poboxes.com
Berkley/Jove and Silhouette

Judith E. French
http://www.randomhouse.com/
catalog/authors/F.html
send SASE: 517 Bridgeville Road,
Seaford, Delaware 19973
Avon Historical and Ballantine

Eve Gaddy
http://www.sff.net/people/Eve.Gaddy
e-mail: e.gaddy1@ballistic.com
P.O. Box 131704, Tyler, TX 75713-1704
Bantam Loveswept

Chevon Gael
e-mail: jacksonk@istar.ca
Red Sage Publishing

Patricia Gaffney
http://www.sff.net/people/PGaffney
e-mail: pgaffney@mail.cvn.net
P.O. Box 672, Blue Ridge Summit, PA 17214
Leisure and Dutton/Signet/Topaz

Linda George (aka Madeline George)
http://www.RomCom.com/george/
e-mail: lindag@eastland.net
P.O. Box 543, Rising Star, Texas 76471
Harlequin Historical

Nancy Gideon
(aka Dana Ransom and Rosalyn West)
http://www.tlt.com/authors/ngideon.htm e-
mail: dana@net-link.net
PO Box 896, Portage, MI 49081
Silhouette and Pinnacle; as Dana Ransom:
Zebra; as Rosalyn West: Avon

Judy Griffith Gill (aka Angie Gaynor)
http://www.sunshine.net/www/0/sn0054
At Canadian Romance Authors Network:
http://www.vgrant.com/cran.htm
e-mail: j_gill@sunshine.net
Bantam Loveswept and Harlequin Love &
Laughter; as Angie Gaynor: Robinson Scarlet

Carol Grace
e-mail: Culvercf@aol.com
Avalon and Silhouette (Romance and Desire)

Elizabeth Graham (aka Laura Parrish)
http://www.tlt.com OR
http://www.kensingtonbooks.com
e-mail: ERGraham@compuserve.com
P.O. Box 63021, Pensacola, Fl, 32526
Zebra Historical; as Laura Parrish:
Avalon Books

Marilyn Grall
http://www.eclectics.com/marilyngrall
e-mail: grall@telepath.com
New Concepts Publishing

Tracy Grant
(aka Anna Grant and Anthea Malcolm)
http://www.tracygrant.org
e-mail: trgrant@tracygrant.org
Dell Historical; as Anna Grant: Zebra
Historical; in collaboration with Joan Grant,
as Anthea Malcolm: Zebra Regency

Vanessa Grant
http://www.vgrant.com
e-mail: vanessa@vgrant.com
Harlequin (Presents, Romance,
and Mills & Boon)
Nonfiction: *Writing Romance,* Self Counsel
Press International

Jennifer Greene (aka Alison Hart, Jeanne Grant, and Jessica Massey)
e-mail: alisonhart@ptn.com
c/o Silhouette Books, 300 E. 42nd St.
New York, NY 10017
Silhouette; as Jeanne Grant: Berkley;
as Jessica Massey: Dell.

Carolyn Greene
e-mail: CarolynGreene@poboxes.com
P.O. Box 412, Powhatan, VA 23139
Harlequin (Romance and Love & Laughter);
as Carolyn Monroe: Silhouette Romance

Shirley Hailstock
http://www.geocities.com/Paris/Bistro/6812
e-mail: Shailstock@prodigy.com
P.O. Box 513, Plainsboro, NJ 08536-0513
Kensington Books

Deborah Hale
http://ourworld.compuserve.com/
homepages/DeborahHale
e-mail: DeborahHale@compuserve.com
Harlequin Historical

Lori Handeland
http://www.eclectics.com/lorihandeland/
Leisure and Love Spell

Kim Hansen (aka Kimberly Greg)
e-mail: iwtbp@execpc.com
P.O. Box 20827, Greenfield, WI 53220-0827
Leisure Historial and Harlequin American; as
Kimberly Greg: Hard Shell Word Factory

Elizabeth Harbison
http://www.sff.net/people/ElizabethHarbison/
e-mail: EHarbison@aol.com
Silhouette Romance

Kathleen Harrington
http://members.aol.com/occauthor/
kathleenharrington
P.O. Box 5511
Hacienda Heights, CA 91745-0511
Avon

Holly Harte (aka Arlene Holliday)
http://www.net-link.net/~hharte
e-mail: hharte@net-link.net
P.O. 384, Paw Paw, MI 49079-0384
Zebra

Robin Lee Hatcher
http://www.robinleehatcher.com
e-mail: robinlee@robinleehatcher.com
P.O. Box 4722, Boise, ID 83711-4722
Avon, Harper Paperbacks, Leisure,
Silhouette, and WaterBrook Press

Lorraine Heath
http://www.paintedrock.com/
authors/heath.htm
e-mail: LorraineHe@aol.com
Avon, Jove, and Topaz

Candice Hern
e-mail: candiceh@informix.com
P.O. Box 13499, San Francisco, CA 94131
Jove and Signet Regency

Rita Herron
e-mail: lherron@mediaone.net
Harlequin (Intrigue and American) and
Precious Gem

Judith Hershner
e-mail: hershner@semo.net
Route 3, Box 341A
Doniphan, Missouri 63935
Kensington Precious Gem

Brenda Hiatt
e-mail: BrendaHB@aol.com
Harlequin (Regency and Superromance) and
Harper Historical

Lisa Higdon
http://www.geocities.com/Heartland/
Acres/8875/
e-mail: LCHigdon@aol.com
P. O. Box 1855, Cordova TN 38088-1855
Jove and Zebra

Tammy Hilz
e-mail: Hilz_Tammy@msn.com
Robinson Scarlet

Metsy Hingle
e-mail: Metsyh@aol.com
http://www.eclectics.com/metsyhingle
PO Box 3224, Covington, LA 70433
Silhouette Desire

Karla Hocker
e-mail: karlahocker2@juno.com
Warner, Walker, and Kensington Publishing

**Jan Hudson (aka Janece O. Hudson, Jan
Oliver, and Ellen Kelly)**
http://www.eclectics.com/janhudson
e-mail: hudson@lcc.net (that's an L, not a 1)
Bantam Loveswept, Dell Candlelight
Supreme, Meteor Kismet, Pinnacle,
Silhouette Desire, and Ballantine/Fawcett

Pamela Ingrahm
e-mail: PaulaDetch@aol.com
Silhouette (Desire and Romance)

Sara Jarrod (Sara Maria Brockunier)
e-mail: Author-Sara@juno.com
P. O. Box 360401
Tampa, Florida 33673-0401
Jove Haunting Hearts, with writing partner

**Sara Jarrod (Ann Josephson, aka Ann
Jacobs)**
http://www.sff.net/people/Ann.Josephson/
index.htm
e-mail: anneric@gte.net
P.O. Box 151596, Tampa, FL 33684-1596
Jove Haunting Hearts with writing partner;
as Ann Jacobs: Red Sage Publishing

Rebecca Kelley
P.O. Box 219234, Portland, OR 97225-9234
Bantam Books–Historical

Dale Ketcham
http://www.romanceweb.com/
dketcham/index.html
e-mail:DaleDK@ix.netcom.com
Kensington Publishing

Mary Kingsley
e-mail: mary.kruger@gte.net
Zebra Regency

Diana Kirk (aka Diana Hart)
http://www.eclectics.com/dianakirk
P.O. Box 31544, Omaha, NE 68131
Hard Shell Word Factory;
as Diana Hart: New Concepts Publishing

Sandra Kitt
http://www.infokart.com/kitt/sandra.html
P.O. Box 403, Planetarium Station
New York 10024-0403
Arabesque, Dutton (Signet & Onyx),
Harlequin American, HarperCollins,
Odyssey Books, and St. Martin's Press

Susan Krinard
http://members.aol.com/skrinard/
e-mail: skrinard@aol.com
P.O. Box 272545, Concord, CA 94527

Lynn Kurland
e-mail: LCurland@aol.com
Berkley

Sylvie Kurtz
e-mail: Kurtzsyl@aol.com
P.O. Box 702, Milford, NH 03055
Leisure Love Spell and Harlequin Intrigue

Allison Lane
http://www.eclectics.com/allisonlane
e-mail: Pace-AllisonLane@worldnet.att.net
Signet Regency

Ann Lawrence
e-mail: annlawrence@pobox.com
P.O. Box 391, Blue Bell, PA 19422
Dorchester Publishing Co., Inc.

Karen Leabo
http://www.dhc.net/~rpreece/author.html
e-mail: leabo@dhc.net
Silhouette (Romance, Desire, and Intimate
Moments) and Bantam Loveswept

Day Leclaire
http://www.geocities.com/Athens/8450
e-mail: leclaire@geocities.com
Harlequin Romance

Catherine Leigh
P.O. Box 774, Ennis, MT 59729
Harlequin Romance

Anne Logan
http://www.eclectics.com/annelogan
P.O. Box 290; Boutte, LA 70039
Harlequin and St. Martin's Press

Jenny Lykins
http://members.aol.com/Lykinsweb/
JennyLykins.html
e-mail: JenLykins@aol.com
P.O. Box 382132
Germantown, TN 38183-2132
Berkley/Jove

Janet Lynnford
http://www.sff.net/people/JanetLynnford
e-mail: jlynnford@aol.com
Topaz

Debbie Macomber
http://www.nettrends.com/debbiemacomber/
P.O. Box 1458, Port Orchard, WA 98366
Harlequin, Harper, Mira,
Silhouette, and Zebra

Jennifer Malin
http://www.geocities.com/Paris/Metro/6890
Berkley/Jove's Time Passages

Tess Mallory
http://members.aol.com/TX4love/
tmallory.html
P.O. Box 316, Wimberley, Texas 78676
Leisure Love Spell

Victoria Malvey
http://www.victoriamalvey.com
e-mail: victoria@victoriamalvey.com
P.O. Box 5069, Clinton, NJ 08809
Pocket Books

Marion Marshall
http://www.eclectics.com/marionmarshall
e-mail: lindass@ipa.net
New Concepts Publishing

Kat Martin
http://www.katbooks.com
e-mail: Katmartin@montana.com
Avon, Berkley, Dell, Kensington, and
St. Martin's Press

Connie Mason
http:/members.aol.com/conmason/index.html
e-mail: ConMason@aol.com
Leisure and Avon

Anne McAllister
e-mail: AnnMcAl@aol.com
Silhouette Desire & Special Edition and
Harlequin (Presents and American)

Pam McCutcheon
http://www.pcisys.net/~pammc/
e-mail: pammc@pcisys.net
Harlequin American, Leisure Love Spell, and
Gryphon Books for Writers

Jenna McKnight
http://www.jennamcknight.com
e-mail: Jenna@jennamcknight.com
P.O. Box 283, Grover, MO 63040-0283
Harlequin (American and Love & Laughter)

Patricia McLinn
http://www.eclectics.com/authorsgalore/
patriciamclinn
e-mail: PMcLinn@aol.com
P.O. Box 7052, Arlington, Va. 22207
Silhouette Special Edition and
Harlequin Historical

Barbara McMahon
http://www.nettrends.com/
barbaramcmahon/
e-mail: bmcmahon@cdepot.net
P.O. Box 977, Pioneer, CA 95666-0977
Harlequin Romance and Silhouette Desire

Suzanne McMinn (aka Suzanne Dye)
http://members.aol.com/suzmcminn
P.O. Box 12, Granbury, TX 76048
Bantam Loveswept, Meteor Kismet,
Silhouette Romance, and Zebra Precious
Gem; as Suzanne Dye: Zebra Precious
Gem

Alisa McNair (aka Lisa McNair Palmer)
http://www.netpage2000.com/romance
e-mail: Lmpwrite@aol.com
Leisure and Greenwood Press

Teresa Medeiros
http://www.win.net/romance/terbio.htm
c/o Bantam Books, 1540 Broadway
New York, NY 10036
Bantam Books

Barbara Metzger
e-mail: BDriftwood@aol.com
Fawcett Regency and Signet Regency

Leigh Michaels
e-mail: leighmichael@lisco.net
P.O. Box 935, Ottumwa, Iowa 52501-0935
Harlequin (Romance and Presents)

Lissa Michaels
http://members.aol.com/LissaMchls/index.html
e-mail: LissaMchls@aol.com
Dreams Unlimited

Sharon Mignerey
http://www.tlt.com/authors/smignry.htm
e-mail: Sharon.Mignerey@worldnet.att.net
Silhouette Intimate Moments and
Zebra

Linda Lael Miller
http://www.booktalk.com/lmiller
P.O. Box 669, Port Orchard, WA 98366
Berkley, Pocket, and Silhouette

Julie Moffett
http://www.writepage.com/authors/
moffettj.htm
e-mail: julie@ei.com
P.O. Box 10001, Alexandria, VA 22310
Leisure

Vickie Moore
e-mail: VickieM22@aol.com
P.O. Box 3967, Wichita, KS 67201
Robinson Scarlet

Peggy Moreland (aka Peggy Morse)
http://www.eclectics.com/peggymoreland
e-mail: peggymoreland@mindspring.com
P.O. Box 2453, Round Rock, TX 78680-2453
Silhouette (Desire and Special Edition); as
Peggy Morse: Meteor Kismet

Kathleen Morgan
e-mail: KMorgan1@aol.com
P.O. Box 62365, Colorado Springs, CO 80962
Dorchester Publishing, Kensington
Publishing, and St. Martin's Press

Melody Morgan
http://www.tlt.com/authors/mmorgan.htm
P.O. Box 155, Swanton, OH 43558
Leisure

Debra Mullins
http://www.wdass.net/dmullins
e-mail: dmullins@wdass.net OR
debmulman@aol.com
P.O. Box 750, Maywood, NJ 07607
Avon Historical

Addison Murray
P.O. Box 1035, Guasti, CA 91743
Kensington Precious Gem

Rina Najman
e-mail: RNJ@Servtech.com
P.O. Box 271 Penfield, NY 14526-0271
Silhouette Intimate Moments

Rachelle Nelson (aka Rachelle Morgan)
http://home1.gte.net/shelinel
e-mail: RachelleNM@juno.com
P.O. Box 1217, Hughes Springs, TX 75656
Jove and Avon

Penelope Neri (aka P.J. Neri)
e-mail: skald@lava.net
Zebra/Kensington, St. Martin's Press,
Leisure Books; as P.J. Neri: The Bess Press

Sara Orwig
http://www.saraorwig.romanticfiction.com
Avon, Bantam, Silhouette (Desire and
Intimate Moments), Harlequin
(Superromance and Regency), Mills & Boon
Historical, Zebra Historical, NAL/Dutton,
Second Chance at Love, Jove, and Warner

Marilyn Pappano
e-mail: pappano@ionet.net
P.O. Box 643, Sapulpa OK 74067-0643
Bantam Books, Silhouette (Intimate Moments
and Special Edition), and Warner

Delia Parr
http://www.geocities.com/SoHo/Lofts/5507/
e-mail: parr@bellatlantic.net
St. Martin's Press

Joanne Pence
http://members.aol.com/jopence
e-mail: jopence@aol.com
P.O. Box 1328, Novato, CA 94948-1328
Harper Monogram

Mary Sharon Plowman
e-mail: sharonplwm@aol.com
Goodfellow Press

Lisa Plumley
http://members.home.com/lplumley
e-mail: lplumley@home.com
Zebra (Historical and Time-travel) and
Kensington Precious Gem

Susan Plunkett
http://www.tlt.com/authors/splunkett.htm
Berkley/Jove

Cheryl Anne Porter
P. O. Box 755, Brandon, FL 33509-0755
Harlequin, St. Martin's Press, and Leisure

Margaret Evans Porter
http://members.aol.com/MargEvaPor
e-mail: MargEvaPor@aol.com
P.O. Box 437, Epsom NH 03234-0437
Avon Historical, Penguin Books/Signet
Regency, Walker & Co.,
Thorndike Press, and Doubleday

Maggie Price
http://members.aol.com/magprice
e-mail: MAGPRICE@aol.com
send SASE: 5208 W. Reno, Suite 350
Oklahoma City, OK 73127
Silhouette Intimate Moments

Mary Jo Putney
http://www.lightst.com/MaryJo/
e-mail: MJP624@aol.com
P.O. Box 243, Riderwood, MD 21139-0243
Penguin Putnam (Signet, Onyx, and Topaz);
Ballantine/Fawcett;
novellas for Kensington and Harlequin

Tara Taylor Quinn
http://www.inficad.com/~ttquinn
e-mail: ttquinn@inficad.com
P.O. Box 15065, Scottsdale, AZ 85267-5065
Harlequin Superromance

Miriam Raftery
e-mail: mraftery@adnc.com OR
mraftery@compuserve.com
fax: (619) 698-7628
Leisure (Love Spell and Anthology)

Francis Ray
http://www.tlt.com/authors/fray.htm
e-mail: FrancisRay@aol.com
Odyssey Books; Kensington (Pinnacle, Denise
Little Presents, and Arabesque)

Emilie Richards
e-mail: ERMcGee@aol.com
P.O. Box 40184, Bay Village, OH 44140
Avon, Harlequin Superromance, Mira, and
Silhouette (Romance, Special Edition, and
Intimate Moments)

Evelyn Richardson
http://www.regency-romance.com
Signet Regency

Connie Rinehold (aka Eve Byron)
http://www.geocities.com/Athens/
Forum/8078/byron.html
e-mail: connierine@aol.com
Harlequin and Dell; as Eve Byron: Avon

Nora Roberts
http://www.lightst.com/nora/
c/o Creative Promotions
344 Cedar Avenue, Ridgewood, NJ 07450
Bantam, Berkley, Harlequin (Historical and
Intrigue), Jove, Mira, Pocket, Putnam, and
Silhouette (Romance, Desire, Special Edition,
and Intimate Moments)

Evelyn Rogers
http://www.romcom.com/rogers
e-mail: 75720.1353@compuserve.com
Avon, Harper, Leisure Love Spell,
and Zebra

**Patricia Rosemoor (aka Lynn Patrick,
Roslynn Patrick, Patrice Lindsey,
and Jeanne Rose)**
http://www.geocities.com/
Athens/Delphi/5100
e-mail: rosemoor@geocities.com
P.O. Box 578297, Chicago, IL 60657-8297
Harlequin Intrigue; as Lynn Patrick
(with writing partner Linda Sweeney): Dell;
as Roslynn Patrick: HarperMonogram; as
Patrice Lindsey: Meteor; as Jeanne Rose:
Silhouette

JoAnn Ross
e-mail: JoAnnRoss@aol.com
HC 31 Box 428, Happy Jack, AZ 86024
Harlequin, NAL, Silhouette, St. Martin's
Press, and Pocket

Renee Roszel
http://www.webzone.net/renee
e-mail: renee@webzone.net
P.O. Box 700154, Tulsa, OK 74170
Harlequin (American, Temptation, Love &
Laughter, and Romance) and Silhouette
(Desire, Special Edition, and Yours Truly)

Patricia Ryan
http://home.eznet.net/~patryan
e-mail: patryan@eznet.net
P.O. Box 26207, Rochester, NY 14626
Dutton/Signet/Topaz and
Harlequin Temptation

Karen Sandler
http://www.innercite.com/~sandler
e-mail: sandler@innercite.com
P.O. Box 165, Rescue, CA 95672
Berkley Haunting Hearts, Kensington
Precious Gem, and Hard Shell Word Factory

Jan Scarbrough
At Kentucky Romance Writers:
http://www.win.net/romance
Kensington Precious Gem

Mary Schramski (aka Mary Starleigh)
e-mail: Schram2@juno.com
Kensington Precious Gem; as Mary Starleigh:
Silhouette Yours Truly

Candace Schuler (aka Jeanette Darwin)
e-mail: Schuler776@msn.com
Harlequin; as Candace Spencer:
Silhouette; as Jeanette Darwin: NAL

Amanda Scott
http://www.geocities.com/Athens/
Forum/8078/scott.html
e-mail: amandascott@worldnet.att.net
P.O. Box 1644, Folsom, CA 95763-1644
Dell, Doubleday, Kensington (Pinnacle and
Zebra), and Penguin USA (Signet)

Martha Shields
e-mail: MarthaShld@aol.com
P.O. Box 240034, Memphis, TN 38124-0034
Silhouette Romance

Lynda Simons
e-mail: simmons@worldchat.com
Silhouette Yours Truly

Rebecca Sinclair
http://www.eclectics.com/rebecca/
e-mail: rsinclair@ids.net
Zebra

Barbara Dawson Smith
http://www.color.net/~bsmith
St. Martin's Press

Marge Smith (aka Elizabeth Sinclair)
http://members.aol.com/ESinclair1/index/html
e-mail: ESinclair1@aol.com
Kensington Precious Gem; as Elizabeth
Sinclair: Silhouette Intimate Moments and
Harlequin American

Maris Soule
http://www.theromanceclub.com/
marissoule.htm
e-mail: soulem@aol.com
P.O. Box 250, Climax, MI 49034
Harlequin (Temptation and Romance),
Silhouette Yours Truly, and Bantam
Loveswept

Lynsey Stevens
e-mail: lynsey@ecn.net.au
Harlequin Presents–Australia

Mariah Stewart
e-mail: MariahStew@aol.com
P. O. Box 481, Lansdowne, PA 19050
Pocket Books

Cheryl St. John
http://www.tlt.com/authors/cstjohn.htm
e-mail: SaintJohn@aol.com
P.O. Box 12142, Florence Station
Omaha, NE 68112-0142
Harlequin (Historical and Silhouette)

Tina St. John
e-mail: TinaStJohn@aol.com
Ballantine Medieval

Deb Stover
http://www.debstover.com/
Kensington, Zebra, and Pinnacle Books

Tracy Sumner
e-mail: Chicago921@aol.com
Zebra Splendor

Myrna Temte
http://pw2.netcom.com/~myrna1/index.htm
e-mail: myrna1@ix.netcom.com
(that's a one, not an el)
Silhouette Special Edition

Shelly Thacker
http://www.shellythacker.com
e-mail: st@shellythacker.com
send SASE: P.O. Box 1022, Novi, MI 48376
Avon Historical and Dell Paranormal

Elizabeth Thornton
http://www.pangea.ca/~thornton
e-mail: thornton@pangea.ca
P.O. Box 69001 RPO Tuxedo Park
Winnipeg MB R3P 2G9 Canada
Bantam, Pinnacle, and Zebra Regency

**Jane Toombs (aka Diana Stuart, Olivia Sumner,
Ellen Jamison, and Jane Anderson)**
http://www.alpine.net/~toombs/
e-mail: toombs@alpine.net
Avon, Ballantine, Berkley, Dell, Harlequin,
Scarlet, Silhouette, Penguin, and Zebra; as
Jane Anderson: Pinnacle

Elizabeth Turner
e-mail: GAOust004@aol.com
Avon, Berkley, Kensington
Publishing, and Pocket

Donna Valentino (aka Julia Hanlon)
e-mail: donnaval@cobweb.net
Harper Monogram, Topaz, Bantam
Loveswept; as Julia Hanlon:
Kensington/Zebra

Joan van Nuys
http://www.eclectics.com/joan
e-mail: jvannuys@infonline.net
P.O. Box 905 Sharon, PA 16146-3428
Avon Books, Leisure, and NAL Rapture

Cynthia Van Rooy
e-mail: cvan@access1.net
Kensington Precious Gem

Lisa Ann Verge
http://www.1q.com/romance/verge
e-mail: LVerge@worldnet.att.net
P.O. Box 43182
Upper Montclair, New Jersey 07043
Kensington, Zebra, and Harlequin

Teresa Warfield
e-mail: TGOkie@aol.com
Berkley Publishing (Diamond,
Jove, Berkley, and Boulevard)

Joanna Wayne
http://www.eclectics.com/
authorsgalore/joannawayne
e-mail: joannawayn@aol.com
P.O. Box 2851, Harvey, LA 70059-2851
Harlequin Intrigue

Ingrid Weaver
e-mail: iweaver@interlog.com
P.O. Box 69035, 12 St. Clair Avenue East
Toronto, Ontario Canada M4T 3A1
Silhouette, Harlequin, and Berkley/Jove

Karen Wiesner
http://members.aol.com/kswiesner/wren.html
e-mail: KSWiesner@aol.com
Hard Shell Word Factory

Susan Wiggs
http://www.poboxes.com/SusanWiggs
e-mail: SusanWiggs@poboxes.com
P.O. Box 4469, Rolling Bay, WA 98061-0469
Avon, Harlequin, HarperCollins, Mira,
PaperJacks, Tor, and Zebra

Denise Dietz Wiley
http://www.eclectics.com/denise
e-mail: DeniDietz@aol.com OR
Calliope97@aol.com
Pinnacle, Hard Shell Word Factory, and
Voices Publishing

Eileen Wilks
e-mail: emwilks@basinlink.com
P.O. Box 4612, Midland, TX 79704-4612
Silhouette (Desire and Intimate Moments)
and St. Martin's Press

Bronwyn Williams
P.O. Box 1028, Buxton, NC 27920
Topaz Historical

Gayle Wilson
e-mail: GAYWILSON@aol.com
P.O. Box 3722, Hueytown, AL 35023
Harlequin (Historical and Intrigue)

Anne Marie Winston
http://www.annemariewinston.com
P.O. Box 302, Zullinger, PA 17272
Silhouette Desire

Cheryl Wolverton
http://www.geocities.com/
Athens/Acropolis/1037
Silhouette and Steeple Hill Love Inspired

Deborah Wood (aka Deborah Lawrence)
http://www.tlt.com/authors/dwood.htm
e-mail: talespinners@wcn.net
Berkley/Jove

Lenora Worth
e-mail: LNwrite@aol.com
Steeple Hill Love Inspired

Writers' Groups

Canadian Romance Writers
http://www.vgrant.com/cran.htm

Kentucky Romance Writers
http://www.win.net/romance

Virginia Romance Writers
http://www.geocities.com/Soho/Museum/2164/

Places To Buy Current And Out-Of-Print Romance Novels

http://www.hardtofindbooks.com

Catalog of hard-to-find books and collectibles. Links to author web sites. Link to *Affaire de Coeur* magazine.

http://www.manderleybooks.com

Manderley Catalog For Romance Readers. Special orders, Romance Bargain of the Week, book search, free catalog.

Open M-F, 7 A.M. - 5 p.m. PST, or call 1-800-301-7546.

http://www.aurorabooks.com

Nice site for romance books.

http://members.aol.com/ttpagebc

Site of the Turn The Page Book Cafe in Maryland. Sells new books in many genres, including romance. Owner of the bookstore cafe is the husband of bestselling author Nora Roberts. Nora will personally sign any of her books you order through this site.

http://www.novelromance.com

Nice site for current romance books. Spotlights featured author/book. Has links to romance sites.

Trade-A-Book

Owners do not have a newsletter or web site yet but they have a large facility with the staff to handle mail order or fax requests for hard-to-find romance novels. They have single titles and series books going back to the beginning of most series, and keep a waiting list if your requested book isn't in stock.

Contact: Kathleen Towne at Trade-A-Book

By mail: 2740 El Camino Real, Santa Clara, CA 95051

By fax: (408) 248-8371

Epilogue

I hope you've enjoyed reading this book and will come back to read it again and again. Above all, keep reading romance novels. In case you haven't noticed, I am a dyed-in-the-wool fan. I love a romantic atmosphere in my home, I devour romance novels, and I adore romantic movies.

I'd love to hear from you. You can reach me in several ways, but be warned, doing so will place you on my mailing list. You'll receive mail from me for years to come.

Victoria M. Johnson
http://www.geocities.com/~victoriajohnsn
e-mail: victoriajohnson@geocities.com
P.O. Box 8562
San Jose, CA 95155